POCKET
CH
SER
KU-649-145

ITALIAN COOKING

Published by Hinkler Books Pty Ltd
45–55 Fairchild Street
Heatherton Victoria 3202 Australia
www.hinkler.com.au

hinkler

Prepress: Splitting Image
Typesetting: MPS Ltd
Design: Pandemonium Creative
© A.C.N. 144 619 894 Pty Ltd 2011

ISBN: 978 1 7418 4099 5

Printed and bound in China

CONTENTS

Introduction   4

Starters   6

Soups   36

Pizza   46

Pasta   56

Risotto and Polenta   100

Mains   114

Dessert   154

Index   174

INTRODUCTION

When you are planning a menu, whether it is for a
dinner party, a casual barbecue or a weeknight family
meal, you should always aim to make it as delicious and
enjoyable as possible. It is important to contrast flavours,
textures and ingredients.

It is an understatement to say that food is important to
the Italians. Meals are prepared with pride and affection
as a daily highlight of family life.

The key to good Italian food is freshness – meals are
cooked with the best quality and freshest ingredients.

Luckily, Italian food is famous for being delicious as well
healthy. Enjoy the benefits of *Pocket Chef Italian Cooking*
on any occasion.

BAKED RICOTTA

Preparation time:
15 minutes + overnight chilling

Total cooking time:
20 minutes

Serves 8

INGREDIENTS

- 1 egg white
- 750 g (1 lb 10 oz) fresh ricotta cheese, well drained
- 60 g (2 oz) sun-dried tomatoes in oil, drained and chopped
- cracked black pepper
- 2 tablespoons chopped flat-leaf parsley
- ½ teaspoon finely grated lemon rind
- 1 clove garlic, crushed
- 1 tablespoon extra virgin olive oil

1 Preheat the oven to 180°C (350°F/Gas 4). Line the base of a 20 cm (8 inch) round shallow cake tin with foil and brush well with olive oil. Beat the egg white with a fork until frothy. Add the ricotta and mix thoroughly. Put half the mixture in the tin and spread evenly over the base. Scatter with the tomato and cracked pepper, spoon the remainder of the ricotta over the top and smooth the surface.

2 Put the parsley, lemon rind and garlic in a bowl and mix well. Sprinkle over the ricotta, top with extra cracked pepper and then drizzle with oil. Brush a circle of foil with oil and place, oil-side-down, over the ricotta. Bake for 20 minutes, or until lightly set. Remove the foil.

3 Leave to cool in the tin, then cover with foil and refrigerate overnight. Carefully turn out onto a tray, remove the foil and then cover with a plate and invert so that the parsley is uppermost. Serve in wedges at room temperature as a starter, garnished with rocket (arugula) leaves and black (ripe) olives, or as part of an antipasto.

HINT: The best way to thoroughly drain ricotta is to leave it in a colander overnight, weighed down with a can or plate. Put a large bowl underneath to catch the liquid.

VARIATION: Try sun-dried capsicum (pepper) instead of tomatoes. Drizzle the oil from the tomatoes or capsicum (pepper) on top, instead of virgin olive oil.

NOTE: Extra virgin olive oil is produced from the first pressing of the olives. Using a superior oil in your cooking makes the difference between a good dish and a great one – always use the best-quality oil you can afford. 'Light' olive oil is from the last pressing and has a very mild flavour.

BRUSCHETTA WITH MEDITERRANEAN TOPPINGS

Preparation time:
20 minutes

Total cooking time:
15 minutes

Serves 4–6

INGREDIENTS

CAPSICUM (PEPPER) TOPPING
- 1 yellow capsicum (pepper)
- 1 red capsicum (pepper)
- 1 green capsicum (pepper)

TOMATO AND BASIL TOPPING
- 2 ripe tomatoes
- ¼ cup (15 g/½ oz) shredded fresh basil
- 1 tablespoon extra virgin olive oil

- 12 slices crusty Italian bread
- 2 cloves garlic, halved
- ⅓ cup (80 ml/2¾ fl oz) extra virgin olive oil
- 1 tablespoon chopped flat-leaf parsley

1 **To make Capsicum (Pepper) Topping:** Cut the capsicums (peppers) in half lengthways and remove the seeds and membrane. Flatten slightly and place, skin-side-up, under a hot grill (broiler) until the skins are blackened. Cover with a tea towel or put the capsicums (peppers) in a paper or plastic bag, seal and leave until cool. Peel away the skins and discard. Slice the flesh into strips.

2 **To make Tomato and Basil Topping:** Finely chop the tomatoes and combine in a bowl with the basil and olive oil. Season with freshly ground black pepper.

3 **To make Bruschetta:** Toast the bread slices and, while still hot, rub with the cut side of a garlic clove. Drizzle olive oil over each slice of bread and sprinkle with salt and plenty of freshly ground black pepper.

4 Arrange the Capsicum (Pepper) Topping on top of half the bread slices; sprinkle with parsley. Arrange the Tomato and Basil Topping on the remaining slices of bread. Serve immediately.

PARMESAN PEARS

Preparation time:
15 minutes

Total cooking time:
10 minutes

Serves 6

INGREDIENTS

- 3 firm ripe pears
- 40 g (1½ oz) butter
- 6 thin slices pancetta,
  finely chopped
- 2 spring (green) onions, finely sliced
- ¾ cup (60 g/2 oz) fresh white
  breadcrumbs
- ⅓ cup (35 g/1¼ oz)
  grated Parmesan

1 Cut the pears in half and remove the cores with a melon baller or teaspoon. Melt the butter in a frying pan. Brush the pears with a little melted butter and place, cut-side-up, on an oven tray (sheet). Put under a preheated grill (broiler) for 4 minutes, or until heated through.

2 Add the pancetta and onions to the remaining butter in the pan. Cook until the onions are soft but not brown. Add the breadcrumbs and black pepper to taste.

3 Scatter the pancetta mixture over the pears, sprinkle with Parmesan and grill until golden brown. Serve warm as a starter, or with roast chicken.

NOTE: Nashi pears are also suitable.

GRAPE AND WALNUT SALAD

Preparation time:
15 minutes + chilling

Total cooking time:
Nil

Serves 6

INGREDIENTS

- 1 butter (Boston) lettuce
- 1 radicchio (red chicory)
- 155 g (5 oz) rocket (arugula)
- 1 cup (185 g/6½ oz) green seedless grapes
- ½ cup (60 g/2 oz) broken walnuts, toasted

DRESSING
- ⅓ cup (80 ml/2¾ fl oz) extra virgin olive oil
- 1 tablespoon lemon juice
- 2 teaspoons wholegrain mustard
- freshly ground black pepper
- 1 tablespoon chopped chives

1 Wash the lettuce, radicchio (red chicory) and rocket (arugula), then dry the leaves gently but thoroughly. Chill until crisp in an airtight container or plastic bag in the refrigerator. Arrange with the grapes in a large salad bowl or serving dish. Scatter with walnuts.

2 **To make Dressing:** Whisk together the oil, lemon juice, mustard and pepper. Add the chives.

3 Drizzle the dressing over the salad and serve.

HINT: Use the best oil you can afford.

VEGETABLE BOATS

Preparation time:
20 minutes

Total cooking time:
45 minutes

Serves 4

INGREDIENTS

* 8 zucchini (courgettes)
* 35 g (1¼ oz) white bread,
  crusts removed
* milk, for soaking
* 125 g (4⅓ oz) ricotta cheese
* 3 tablespoons grated Cheddar
  (American) cheese
* ⅓ cup (35 g/1¼ oz)
  grated Parmesan
* 2 teaspoons chopped fresh oregano
* 2 teaspoons chopped fresh thyme
* 1 clove garlic, crushed
* 1 egg yolk

1 Preheat the oven to moderately
hot 190°C (375°F/Gas 5).
Cook the zucchini (courgettes)
in boiling salted water for
5 minutes, then drain.
Meanwhile, soak the bread in
milk until soft, then squeeze dry.
Cut the zucchini (courgettes) in
half and scoop out the flesh with
a teaspoon.

2 Chop the zucchini (courgette)
flesh finely. Place in a bowl and
add the bread, cheeses, herbs,
garlic and egg yolk, and season
with salt and pepper. Mix
together, adding a little milk
to make it bind together
if necessary.

3 Fill the zucchini (courgette)
shells with the stuffing. Brush
an ovenproof baking dish with
oil and arrange the zucchini
(courgettes) close together. Bake
in the oven for 35–40 minutes,
until golden on top. Serve
immediately.

SPINACH AND PANCETTA PIE

Preparation time:
30 minutes

Total cooking time:
55 minutes

Serves 4–6

INGREDIENTS

- 45 g (1⅔ oz) butter
- 2 tablespoons olive oil
- 1 large onion, finely chopped
- 2 cloves garlic, finely chopped
- 125 g (4⅓ oz) finely sliced pancetta, chopped
- 1 cup (220 g/7¾ oz) arborio rice
- 3 cups (750 ml/26 fl oz) beef stock (broth)
- 800 g (1 lb 12 oz) English (common) spinach, coarsely chopped
- 4 eggs, lightly beaten
- ½ cup (50 g/1¾ oz) freshly grated Parmesan
- 1 teaspoon coarsely cracked black pepper
- 4 tablespoons dry breadcrumbs

1 Heat the butter and 1 tablespoon oil in a large frying pan and cook the onion for 3–4 minutes. Add the garlic and pancetta and cook for 1 minute.

2 Add the rice and stir to coat. Pour in half the stock (broth), reduce the heat, cover and simmer for 8 minutes, adding the remaining stock (broth) gradually as it is absorbed. Continue cooking the rice until all the stock (broth) has been absorbed. Preheat the oven to moderate 180°C (350°F/Gas 4).

3 Fold the spinach into the rice, cover and simmer for a further 2 minutes, or until just wilted. Transfer to a bowl and leave to cool a little. Stir in the eggs, Parmesan and cracked pepper.

4 Sprinkle a greased 23 cm (9 inch) springform tin with 3 tablespoons of the breadcrumbs. Spoon in the filling, drizzle with the remaining oil and sprinkle the remaining breadcrumbs over the top. Bake

for 40–45 minutes, then cool in the tin. Cut into wedges and serve at room temperature.

NOTE: Ready-made stock (broth) is very good but can be salty – use half stock (broth), half water.

FISH AND VEGETABLE ROLLS

Preparation time:
20 minutes + 30 minutes marinating

Total cooking time:
10 minutes

Serves 6

INGREDIENTS

- 2 large red capsicums (peppers)
- 2 large yellow capsicums (peppers)
- 2 large green capsicums (peppers)
- 3 tablespoons olive oil
- 1 teaspoon lemon juice
- 2 cloves garlic, crushed
- 185 g (6½ oz) flaked tuna, drained
- 100 g (3½ oz) anchovies, drained and chopped
- ⅓ cup (60 g/2 oz) black (ripe) olives, pitted and chopped
- 2 tablespoons capers, drained
- 1 tablespoon chopped fresh parsley

1 Cut the capsicums (peppers) into quarters lengthways, remove the seeds and membrane and brush the skin with a little of the oil. Cook until a hot grill (broiler), skin-side-up, until the skins are black and blistered. Cover with a tea towel and leave to cool. Peel away the skin.

2 Combine the remaining oil, lemon juice, garlic and a little salt. Marinate the capsicums (peppers) in this for 30 minutes. In another bowl, mix together the tuna, anchovies, olives and capers.

3 Drain the capsicums (peppers), reserving the marinade, and place 2 teaspoons of tuna filling on each piece. Roll up and arrange on a serving dish. Drizzle with the reserved marinade and then garnish with chopped parsley and cracked black pepper.

CAPONATA

Preparation time:
25 minutes

Total cooking time:
35 minutes

Serves 6

INGREDIENTS

- 3 tablespoons olive oil
- 2 onions, sliced
- 2 red capsicums (peppers),
  thinly sliced
- 4 cloves garlic, finely chopped
- 4 celery sticks (ribs), sliced
- 1 large eggplant (aubergine)
  (500 g/1 lb 2 oz), cubed
- 1 kg (2 lb 3 oz) fresh tomatoes,
  peeled and chopped
- 2 tablespoons fresh thyme leaves
- 2 tablespoons sugar
- ½ cup (125 ml/4¼ fl oz)
  red wine vinegar
- 125 g (4¼ oz) pitted green olives,
  rinsed well and drained
- 2 tablespoons capers, drained

1 Heat the oil in a large frying pan and add the onion, capsicum (pepper), garlic, celery and eggplant (aubergine). Cover and then leave to simmer over low heat for 20 minutes. Season to taste with salt and freshly ground black pepper.

2 Add the tomatoes and thyme and leave to simmer, uncovered, for a further 15 minutes.

3 Add the sugar, vinegar, olives and capers to the vegetables and mix well. Taste and season again if necessary before serving. Serve warm or at room temperature.

HINT: Peel fresh tomatoes by scoring a cross in the top of the tomato and placing in a bowl of boiling water for 1 minute. Plunge into cold water and peel the skin away from the cross.

NOTE: Green olives are picked and processed when they are unripe.

ASPARAGUS WITH PARMESAN

Preparation time:
15 minutes

Total cooking time:
10 minutes

Serves 4

INGREDIENTS

- 60 g (2 oz) butter
- 2 tablespoons grated
  fresh Parmesan
- ½ cup (40 g/1½ oz) fresh
  breadcrumbs
- 2 tablespoons pine nuts, chopped
- 1 clove garlic, finely chopped
- 2 teaspoons chopped fresh oregano
- 2 teaspoons chopped fresh
  flat-leaf parsley
- freshly ground black pepper
- 500 g (1 lb 2 oz) fresh asparagus
- 60 g (2 oz) butter, melted,
  for serving

1 Heat the butter in a pan and, when foaming, add the Parmesan cheese, breadcrumbs and pine nuts. Stir over medium heat until lightly browned and crisp, then add the garlic, herbs and pepper, and mix well.

2 Boil, steam or microwave the asparagus for 2–3 minutes, or until just tender, then rinse under cold water and pat dry with paper towels.

3 Serve the asparagus immediately, sprinkled with the crisp Parmesan topping and drizzled with extra melted butter.

NOTE: Use slightly stale bread to make breadcrumbs in a processor.

BAKED MUSHROOMS

Preparation time:
15 minutes

Total cooking time:
15 minutes

Serves 4

INGREDIENTS

- 250 g (8¾ oz) button mushrooms
- 200 g (7 oz) oyster mushrooms
- 200 g (7 oz) shiitake mushrooms
- 100 g (3⅓ oz) Swiss brown mushrooms

TOPPING
- 1 cup (80 g/2¾ oz) fresh breadcrumbs
- ¼ cup (25 g/¾ oz) freshly grated Parmesan
- 2 tablespoons chopped fresh flat-leaf parsley
- 1 tablespoon chopped fresh thyme
- 2 cloves garlic, crushed
- 1 teaspoon cracked pepper
- 2 tablespoons extra virgin olive oil

1 Preheat the oven to moderate 180°C (350°F/Gas 4). Wipe the mushrooms with damp paper towel. Trim away the hard tips and discard. Cut any large mushrooms in half lengthways.

2 Sprinkle the base of a large baking dish with a little water. Place the mushrooms in a single layer in the dish, stems upwards.

3 **To make Topping:** Mix together the breadcrumbs, Parmesan, herbs, garlic and pepper, sprinkle over the mushrooms and drizzle with oil. Bake for 12–15 minutes and serve warm.

NOTE: Use day-old bread which is slightly stale to make breadcrumbs. Simply remove the crusts and chop in a food processor until crumbs form.

HINT: Wipe mushrooms clean with a damp paper towel. They can be rinsed in a colander if necessary but avoid soaking them because this will make them soggy.

CHEESE AND SPINACH PANCAKES

Preparation time:
40 minutes

Total cooking time:
50 minutes

Serves 4

INGREDIENTS

- 250 g (8¾ oz) cooked, drained English (common) spinach, chopped
- ½ cup (125 g/4⅓ oz) ricotta cheese
- ¼ cup (30 g/1 oz) grated Cheddar (American) cheese
- ground black pepper
- freshly grated nutmeg
- ¼ cup (25 g/¾ oz) grated Parmesan
- ½ teaspoon paprika
- ½ cup (40 g/1½ oz) fresh breadcrumbs

BATTER
- 1 cup (125 g/4⅓ oz) plain (all-purpose) flour
- 1¼ cups (315 ml/11 fl oz) milk
- 1 egg
- butter, for cooking

CHEESE SAUCE
- 2 tablespoons butter
- ¼ cup (30 g/1 oz) plain (all-purpose) flour
- 1¾ cups (440 ml/15 fl oz) milk
- 1 cup (125 g/4⅓ oz) grated Cheddar (American) cheese

1 Put the spinach, cheeses, pepper and nutmeg in a bowl and mix well.

2 **To make Batter:** Sift the flour and a pinch of salt into a bowl. Add half the milk and the egg. Whisk until smooth; add

the remaining milk. Heat a teaspoon of butter in a frying pan and pour in a thin layer of batter. Cook the base until golden, then flip. The batter should make 8 pancakes.

3 **To make Cheese Sauce:** Melt
the butter over low heat, add the
flour and cook for 1 minute.
Remove from the heat and slowly
stir in the milk. Bring to the boil,
stirring constantly. Remove from
the heat and add salt and pepper,
and the grated cheese.

4 Preheat the oven to 180°C
(350°F/Gas 4). Divide the filling
among the pancakes, roll up and
put in a greased ovenproof dish.
Pour Cheese Sauce over the
pancakes. Mix the Parmesan,
paprika and breadcrumbs
together and sprinkle over the
sauce. Bake for 30 minutes, or
until golden brown.

FENNEL WITH PECORINO CHEESE

Preparation time:
15 minutes

Total cooking time:
25 minutes

Serves 4

INGREDIENTS

- 4 fennel bulbs
- 1 clove garlic, crushed
- ½ lemon, sliced
- 2 tablespoons olive oil
- 1 teaspoon salt
- 3 tablespoons butter, melted
- 2 tablespoons grated pecorino cheese

1 Cut the top shoots and base off the fennel and remove the tough outer layers. Cut into segments and place in a pan with the garlic, lemon, oil and salt. Cover with water and bring to the boil. Reduce the heat and simmer for 20 minutes, or until just tender.

2 Drain well and place in a heatproof dish. Drizzle with the butter. Sprinkle with the cheese and season with salt and pepper to taste.

3 Place under a preheated grill (broiler) until the cheese has browned. Best served immediately.

NOTE: If pecorino (a hard sheep's milk cheese) is not available, then use Parmesan instead.

MUSHROOMS IN TOMATO SAUCE

Preparation time:
15 minutes

Total cooking time:
20 minutes

Serves 4

INGREDIENTS

- 2 tablespoons olive oil
- 2 cloves garlic, sliced
- 600 g (1 lb 5 oz) large button mushrooms, halved
- 2 tablespoons tomato paste (tomato puree)
- 2 tablespoons chopped fresh marjoram
- 250 g (8¾ oz) cherry tomatoes, halved
- freshly ground black pepper
- 1 tablespoon chopped fresh oregano leaves

1 Heat the oil in a pan, add the garlic and stir over moderate heat for 1 minute; do not brown.

2 Add the mushrooms and cook, stirring, for 5 minutes, until combined and beginning to soften.

3 Stir through the tomato paste (tomato puree), marjoram and cherry tomatoes, and cook over low heat until the mushrooms are soft. Serve sprinkled with pepper and oregano leaves.

NOTE: Can be made up to two days ahead and served hot or cold.

WHITEBAIT FRITTERS

Preparation time:
20 minutes + resting

Total cooking time:
15 minutes

Makes 10

INGREDIENTS

- ¼ cup (30 g/1 oz) self-raising flour
- ¼ cup (30 g/1 oz) plain (all-purpose) flour
- ½ teaspoon bicarbonate of soda (baking soda)
- 1 teaspoon salt
- freshly ground black pepper
- 1 egg, lightly beaten
- 3 tablespoons dry white wine
- 2 teaspoons chopped fresh flat-leaf parsley
- 1 clove garlic, crushed
- ½ small onion, grated
- 200 g (7 oz) Chinese or New Zealand whitebait
- olive oil, for shallow frying
- lemon wedges, to serve

1 Sift the flours, bicarbonate of soda (baking soda), salt and pepper into a bowl. Stir through the egg and wine, whisk until smooth, then add the parsley, garlic, onion and whitebait. Cover and leave for 20 minutes.

2 Heat the oil in a frying pan and then drop in tablespoons of batter. When the batter is puffed and bubbles appear on the surface, carefully turn to cook the other side.

3 Drain on paper towels and serve immediately with lemon wedges.

NOTE: Chinese or New Zealand whitebait are very small and fine, and can be bought fresh or frozen.

STUFFED SARDINES

Preparation time:
40 minutes

Total cooking time:
20 minutes

Serves 4

INGREDIENTS

- 8 large sardines
- 1/3 cup (35 g/1 1/4 oz) dry breadcrumbs
- 1 clove garlic, crushed
- 1 tablespoon capers, finely chopped
- 2 tablespoons grated fresh Parmesan
- freshly ground black pepper
- 1 egg yolk, lightly beaten
- juice of 1 lemon, to serve

1 Preheat the oven to moderately hot 200°C (400°F/Gas 6). Lightly grease an oven tray (sheet).

2 Remove the heads from the sardines, make a slit through the gut and open out flat. Remove the guts and carefully scrape the flesh away from the backbone; trim at the tail end leaving the tail intact. Lift out the backbone; discard. Wash the sardines well and drain on paper towels.

3 Mix together the breadcrumbs, garlic, capers, Parmesan, pepper and enough egg yolk to bind the stuffing together. Spoon a little onto each open sardine, put on the oven tray (sheet) and bake for 20 minutes, until golden. Serve drizzled with lemon juice.

NOTE: You can buy sardines already filleted from some fishmongers. This makes the recipe quick and simple.

SEAFOOD SOUP

Preparation time:
40 minutes

Total cooking time:
1 hour 40 minutes

Serves 6

INGREDIENTS

- 800 g (1 lb 12 oz) baby octopus
- 155 g (5½ oz) small cleaned calamari tubes
- 500 g (1 lb 2 oz) firm fish fillets
- 12 small mussels in shells
- 1 tablespoon olive oil
- 2 small onions, sliced
- 1 anchovy fillet, finely chopped
- 3 large ripe tomatoes, skinned and finely chopped
- 3 fresh mint leaves, torn
- 2 bay leaves
- ½ cup (125 ml/4¼ fl oz) dry white wine
- 315 g (11¼ oz) frozen peas

- 12 raw king prawns (shrimp), shelled and deveined with tails intact
- 2 tablespoons lemon juice

GARLIC BREAD
- 6 slices crusty Italian bread
- 1 clove garlic, halved

PARSLEY PESTO
- 1 cup (20 g/⅔ oz) firmly packed flat-leaf parsley leaves
- 2 cloves garlic, chopped
- 2 tablespoons lemon juice
- 2 tablespoons olive oil

1 Remove the heads and beaks from the octopus and cut the tentacles into smaller portions. Cut the calamari tubes into rings. Put the octopus in a large pan of boiling water, partially cover the pan and leave to simmer for 30 minutes. Add the calamari rings and simmer for 15–20 minutes, or until tender. Drain thoroughly.

2 Cut the fish fillets into bite-sized portions. Scrub the mussel shells

and remove their beards. Refrigerate all the seafood on separate plates.

3 Heat the oil in a large pan and cook the onion over moderate heat until starting to colour. Stir in the anchovy, tomatoes, mint and bay leaves, wine, 1.5 litres (1.6 US qt/1.3 UK qt) water, and salt and pepper, to taste. Bring to the boil, lower the heat and simmer for 20 minutes.

4 **To make Garlic Bread:** Preheat the oven to 160°C (315°F/ Gas 2–3). Put the bread on a baking tray (sheet) in a single layer. Bake for 20 minutes, or until crisp, turning once. Rub each slice of bread with the cut garlic.

5 **To make Parsley Pesto:** Put the parsley, garlic, lemon juice and olive oil in a food processor. Process into a fine paste and season to taste with salt and pepper. Cover and refrigerate until ready to serve.

6 Just before serving, bring the soup back to the boil and add the peas, mussels and fish. Reduce the heat to simmer, uncovered, for 3 minutes or until the mussels start to open. Add the prawns (shrimp), octopus and calamari. Bring back to the boil, then reduce the heat and simmer for 2–3 minutes, or until all the seafood is tender. Stir in the lemon juice and discard any unopened mussels. Place a slice of Garlic Bread in each serving bowl and ladle Seafood Soup over the top. Serve the Parsley Pesto separately.

NOTE: To remove the beak from the octopus, turn the head inside out and push the beak (the dark hard bit) up firmly – it will pop out. The seafood, stock (broth) and bread can all be prepared a few hours in advance and the soup completed just before serving.

MINESTRONE

Preparation time:
30 minutes + overnight soaking

Total cooking time:
2 hours 45 minutes

Serves 6–8

INGREDIENTS

* 250 g (8¾ oz) dried borlotti (romano) beans
* 2 tablespoons oil
* 2 onions, chopped
* 2 cloves garlic, crushed
* 3 rashers bacon, chopped
* 4 egg tomatoes, peeled and chopped
* 3 tablespoons chopped parsley
* 9 cups (2.25 litres/2.4 US qt/ 2 UK qt) beef or vegetable stock (broth)
* 3 tablespoons red wine
* 1 carrot, peeled and chopped
* 1 swede (yellow turnip/rutabaga), peeled and diced
* 2 potatoes, peeled and diced
* 3 tablespoons tomato paste (tomato puree)
* 2 zucchini (courgettes), sliced
* ½ cup (80 g/2¾ oz) peas
* ½ cup (80 g/2¾ oz) small macaroni
* Parmesan and pesto, to serve

1 Soak the borlotti (romano) beans in water overnight and drain. Add to a pan of boiling water, simmer for 15 minutes and drain. Heat the oil in a large heavy-based pan and cook the onion, garlic and bacon, stirring, until the onion is soft and the bacon golden.

2 Add the tomato, parsley, borlotti (romano) beans, stock (broth) and red wine. Simmer, covered, over low heat for 2 hours. Add the carrot, swede (yellow turnip/ rutabaga), potato and tomato paste (tomato puree), cover and simmer for a further 15–20 minutes.

3 Add the zucchini (courgette), peas and pasta. Cover and simmer for 10–15 minutes, or until the vegetables and macaroni are tender. Season to taste with salt and pepper, and serve topped with grated Parmesan and a little pesto.

BROCCOLI AND PINE NUT SOUP

Preparation time:
10 minutes

Total cooking time:
30 minutes

Serves 6

INGREDIENTS

- 30 g (1 oz) butter
- 1 onion, finely chopped
- 6 cups (1.5 litres/1.6 US qt/ 1.3 UK qt) chicken stock (broth)
- 750 g (1 lb 10 oz) fresh broccoli
- ⅓ cup (50 g/1¾ oz) pine nuts
- extra pine nuts, to serve

1 Melt the butter in a large pan and cook the onion over moderate heat until soft but not browned. Add the stock (broth) and bring to the boil.

2 Remove the florets from the broccoli and set aside. Chop the broccoli stalks and add to the pan. Reduce the heat, cover and simmer for 15 minutes. Add the florets and simmer, uncovered, for 10 minutes, or until the florets are tender. Allow to cool completely.

3 Add the pine nuts and blend until smooth in a food processor (you may need to blend in batches, depending on the size of your processor). Season to taste with salt and pepper, then gently reheat. Sprinkle with extra pine nuts to serve. Delicious with toasted foccacia, drizzled with extra virgin olive oil.

PUMPKIN AND BEAN SOUP

Preparation time:
20 minutes + overnight soaking

Total cooking time:
2 hours 10 minutes

Serves 4–6

INGREDIENTS

- 350 g (12¼ oz) dried borlotti (romano) beans
- 1 kg (2 lb 3 oz) butternut pumpkin (squash) pieces, skin and seeds removed
- 2 large potatoes, peeled and chopped
- 2 litres (2.1 US qt/1.75 UK qt) chicken stock (broth)
- 1 tablespoon olive oil
- 1 red onion, chopped
- 2 cloves garlic, finely chopped
- 1 celery stick (rib), sliced
- 10 fresh sage leaves, chopped
- ½ teaspoon finely cracked black pepper

1 Soak the beans in cold water overnight or for 8 hours, then rinse and drain. Put in a large saucepan, cover with water and simmer over gentle heat for 1½ hours, or until tender. Remove and drain.

2 Place the pumpkin (squash) and potato pieces in a large saucepan and pour in the chicken stock (broth). Bring to the boil, then reduce the heat and simmer for 35–40 minutes, or until soft. Remove from the heat and drain, reserving the liquid. Roughly mash the pumpkin (squash) and potatoes with a fork, then return to the pan with the reserved liquid. Stir in the beans.

3 Heat the oil in a small frying pan, add the onion, garlic and celery and fry for 2–3 minutes. Add to the soup with the sage and pepper and heat through. Serve hot with crusty Italian bread.

HINT: Ready-made chicken stock (broth) is very convenient but can be salty – use half stock (broth), half water.

TOMATO DITALINI SOUP

Preparation time:
15 minutes

Cooking time:
20-minutes

Serves 4

INGREDIENTS

- 2 tablespoons olive oil
- 1 large onion, finely chopped
- 2 celery sticks (ribs), finely chopped
- 3 vine-ripened tomatoes
- 6 cups (1.5 litres / 1.6 US qt / 1.3 UK qt) chicken or vegetable stock (broth)
- 90 g (3¼ oz) ditalini
- 2 tablespoons chopped fresh flat-leaf (Italian) parsley

1 Heat the oil in a large saucepan over medium heat. Add the onion and celery and cook for 5 minutes, or until they have softened.

2 Score a cross in the base of each tomato, then place in a bowl of boiling water for 1 minute. Plunge into cold water and peel the skin away from the cross. Halve the tomatoes and scoop out the seeds. Roughly chop the flesh. Add the stock (broth) and tomato to the onion mixture and bring to the boil. Add the pasta and cook for 10 minutes, or until *al dente*. Season and sprinkle with parsley.

POTATO ONION PIZZA

Preparation time:
40 minutes

Total cooking time:
40 minutes

Serves 4

INGREDIENTS

- 7 g (¼ oz) sachet dry yeast
- ½ teaspoon sugar
- 1½ cups (185 g/6½ oz) plain (all-purpose) flour
- 1 cup (150 g/5¼ oz) wholemeal plain (whole wheat all-purpose) flour
- 1 tablespoon olive oil

TOPPING
- 1 large red capsicum (pepper)
- 1 potato, peeled
- 1 large onion, sliced
- 125 g (4⅓ oz) soft goat's cheese, crumbled
- 3 tablespoons capers
- 1 tablespoon dried oregano
- 1 teaspoon cracked pepper
- 1 teaspoon olive oil

1 Mix the yeast, sugar, a good pinch of salt and 1 cup (250 ml/8½ fl oz) warm water in a bowl. Cover with plastic wrap and leave in a warm place for 10 minutes, or until foamy. Sift both flours into a bowl. Make a well in the centre, add the yeast mixture and mix to a firm dough. Knead on a lightly floured surface for 5 minutes, or until smooth. Roll out to a 35 cm (14 inch) round. Brush a 30 cm (12 inch) pizza tray (sheet) with oil; put the dough on the tray (sheet) and tuck the edge over to form a rim. Preheat the oven to moderately hot 200°C (400°F/Gas 6).

2 **To make Topping:** Cut the capsicum (pepper) into large flat pieces; remove the seeds. Place, skin-side-up, under a hot grill (broiler) until blackened. Cool under a tea towel, peel away the skin and cut the flesh into narrow strips.

3 Slice the potato paper thin and arrange over the base with the onion, capsicum (pepper) and half the goat's cheese. Sprinkle with capers, oregano and pepper and drizzle with olive oil. Brush the edge of the crust with oil and bake for 20 minutes. Add the remaining goat's cheese and bake for 15–20 minutes, or until the crust has browned. Cut into wedges to serve.

NOTE: Goat's cheese, also known as Chèvre, is available at delicatessens.

SUN-DRIED TOMATO AND SALAMI PIZZA

Preparation time:
40 minutes

Total cooking time:
35–45 minutes

Serves 4

INGREDIENTS

- 1 green capsicum (pepper)
- 1 red or yellow capsicum (pepper)
- 1 cup (125 g/4⅓ oz) grated Cheddar (American) cheese
- 100 g (3½ oz) salami, sliced
- 1 red onion, thinly sliced into rings
- ½ cup (90 g/3¼ oz) black (ripe) olives, pitted and sliced
- 150 g (5¼ oz) bocconcini

PIZZA BASE
- 7 g (¼ oz) sachet dried yeast
- ½ teaspoon salt
- ½ teaspoon sugar
- 2½ cups (250 g/8¾ oz) plain (all-purpose) flour
- 1 cup (160 g/5⅔ oz) sun-dried tomatoes, finely chopped
- ½ cup (80 g/2¾ oz) pine nuts, finely chopped

1 Cut the capsicums (peppers) into large flat pieces; remove the membrane and seeds. Place, skin-side-up, under a hot grill (broiler) and cook until the skin blackens and blisters. Cool under a tea towel. Peel away the skin and cut the flesh into thin strips. Set aside.

2 **To make Pizza Base:** Mix the yeast, salt, sugar and 1 cup (250 ml/8½ fl oz) warm water in a small bowl. Cover with plastic wrap and leave in a warm place for 10 minutes, until foamy. Sift the flour into a bowl, make a well in the centre and add the yeast mixture, sun-dried tomatoes and pine nuts. Mix to a dough.

3 Preheat the oven to moderately hot 200°C (400°F/Gas 6). Knead the dough on a lightly floured surface for about 10 minutes, or until smooth and elastic. Roll out to a 35 cm (14 inch) round. Place on a 30 cm (12 inch) non-stick pizza tray (sheet), folding the edge over to form a rim.

4 Sprinkle the pizza base with grated cheese. Top with salami, red onion, olives and roasted capsicum (pepper). Bake for 30–40 minutes, or until the base is cooked. Top with thinly sliced bocconcini and bake for a further 5 minutes, or until just melted.

VARIATION: Use sun-dried capsicum (pepper) instead of tomato in the pizza base.

OLIVE AND ONION TART

Preparation time:
25 minutes

Total cooking time:
35–40 minutes

Serves 4–6

INGREDIENTS

- 1 teaspoon sugar
- 1½ teaspoons dried yeast
- ½ cup (125 ml/4¼ fl oz) olive oil
- 5 onions, thinly sliced
- 1 cup (125 g/4⅓ oz)
  self-raising flour
- ½ cup (125 g/4⅓ oz) plain
  (all-purpose) white flour
- 1 cup (185 g/6½ oz) black
  (ripe) olives
- 2 tablespoons grated
  Parmesan cheese

1 Dissolve the sugar in ½ cup (125 ml/4¼ fl oz) warm water. Sprinkle with yeast and leave for 10 minutes, or until frothy.

2 Heat 3 tablespoons oil in a frying pan and fry the onion for 10 minutes, or until soft. Leave to cool. Preheat the oven to hot 220°C (425°F/Gas 7).

3 Sift together the self-raising flour, plain (all-purpose) flour and a good pinch of salt in a bowl. Make a well in the centre and pour in the yeast mixture and 2 tablespoons oil. Bring together to form a dough and knead on a lightly floured surface for 10 minutes, or until smooth. Extra flour may be necessary.

4 Roll out the dough to line a greased 30 cm (12 inch) pizza tray (sheet). Spread with cooked onions, then olives. Brush the crust with the remaining olive oil. Bake for 25–30 minutes. Serve hot or cold, sprinked with grated Parmesan.

HAM AND CHEESE CALZONE

Preparation time:
30 minutes + chilling

Total cooking time:
30 minutes

Makes 4

INGREDIENTS

- 2 cups (250 g/8¾ oz) plain (all-purpose) flour
- 100 g (3½ oz) butter, chopped
- 2 egg yolks

HAM AND CHEESE FILLING
- 250 g (8¾ oz) ricotta cheese
- 50 g (1¾ oz) Gruyère cheese, cubed
- 50 g (1¾ oz) ham, finely chopped
- 2 spring (green) onions, chopped
- 1 tablespoon chopped fresh flat-leaf parsley
- freshly ground black pepper

1 Lightly grease a large oven tray (sheet). Sift the flour and a pinch of salt into a bowl and rub in the butter. Make a well in the centre, cut in the egg yolks with a knife and add 2–3 tablespoons water, or enough to form a dough. Gather together into a ball, cover with plastic wrap and chill for 20 minutes. Preheat the oven to moderately hot 200°C (400°F/ Gas 6).

2 **To make Filling:** Combine the cheeses, ham, spring (green) onions, parsley and black pepper in a bowl.

3 Roll out a quarter of the dough to make a large round 3 mm (⅛ inch) thick, trimming any uneven edges. Spoon a quarter of the filling mixture into the centre, brush the edge very lightly with water and fold over to enclose the filling, pressing the edge to seal. Repeat with the remaining dough and filling. Place the Calzone on the oven tray (sheet), brush with a little olive oil and bake for 30 minutes, or until well browned and crisp.

NOTE: Calzone can be made 1 day ahead and kept refrigerated before baking. Pastry can be made in a food processor, in short bursts.

ROASTED TOMATO AND OREGANO PIZZA

Preparation time:
40 minutes

Total cooking time:
1 hour 45 minutes

Serves 4

INGREDIENTS

- 500 g (1 lb 2 oz) plum (egg-shaped) tomatoes
- 1 large eggplant (aubergine)
- olive oil, for frying
- 200 g (7 oz) mozzarella, grated
- ¼ cup (25 g/¾ oz) grated Parmesan
- 1 tablespoon chopped fresh oregano

PIZZA BASE
- 1 teaspoon dried yeast
- ¼ teaspoon salt
- ¼ teaspoon sugar
- 1¼ cups (155 g/5½ oz) plain (all-purpose) flour
- 6 cloves garlic, crushed

1 Preheat the oven to slow 150°C (300°F/Gas 2). Cut the tomatoes in half and place in one layer on a baking tray (sheet), cut-side-up. Sprinkle with salt and roast for 1 hour 15 minutes. Set aside to cool.

2 **To make Pizza Base:** Put the yeast, salt, sugar and ½ cup (125 ml/4¼ fl oz) warm water in a small bowl. Leave, covered with plastic wrap, in a warm place for 10 minutes, or until foamy. Sift the flour into a large bowl, make a well in the centre and add the yeast mixture and garlic. Mix to form a dough. Knead on a lightly floured surface for 10 minutes, or until smooth and elastic. Roll out to fit a 30 cm (12 inch) greased or non-stick pizza tray (sheet).

3 Preheat the oven to moderately hot 200°C (400°F/Gas 6). Thinly slice the eggplant (aubergine). Drizzle a char-grill (char-broiler) or large frying pan with olive oil until nearly smoking. Add the eggplant (aubergine) in batches and cook, turning once, until soft (brush with a little more oil if it starts to stick). Drain on paper towels.

4 Arrange the eggplant
(aubergine) on the pizza base.
Top with tomatoes and sprinkle
with the combined mozzarella
and Parmesan. Bake for
20–30 minutes, or until the base
is cooked and the cheese melted
and golden. Sprinkle with fresh
oregano to serve.

SPAGHETTI BOLOGNESE

Preparation time:
10 minutes

Cooking time:
55 minutes

Serves 4

INGREDIENTS

- 1 tablespoon olive oil
- 1 large onion, diced
- 2 garlic cloves, crushed
- 600 g (1 lb 5 oz) minced (ground) beef
- ½ cup (125 ml/4¼ fl oz) red wine
- ½ cup (125 ml/4¼ fl oz) beef stock (broth)
- 2 × 400 g (14 oz) cans chopped tomatoes
- 1 carrot, grated
- 350 g (12¼ oz) spaghetti

1 Heat the oil over medium heat in a large saucepan, add the onion and garlic and cook for 1–2 minutes, or until soft. Add the meat and cook, stirring to break up any lumps, for 5 minutes, or until the meat is browned. Pour in the wine and simmer for 2–3 minutes, or until reduced slightly, then add the stock (broth) and simmer for 2 minutes. Add the tomato and carrot and season well. Cook over low heat for 40 minutes.

2 About 15 minutes before serving, cook the pasta in a large saucepan of boiling water until *al dente*. Drain well and keep warm. Divide the pasta evenly among four serving bowls and pour the meat sauce over the pasta. Garnish with parsley, if desired.

HINT: Delicious with grated Parmesan cheese.

PASTA GNOCCHI WITH SAUSAGE

Preparation time:
15 minutes

Cooking time:
20 minutes

Serves 4–6

INGREDIENTS

- 500 g (1 lb 2 oz) pasta gnocchi
- 2 tablespoons olive oil
- 400 g (14 oz) thin Italian sausages
- 1 red onion, finely chopped
- 2 garlic cloves, finely chopped
- 2 × 400 g (14 oz) cans chopped tomatoes
- 1 teaspoon caster (berry) sugar
- 35 g (1¼ oz) fresh basil, torn
- ½ cup (45 g/1⅓ oz) grated pecorino cheese

1 Cook the pasta in a large saucepan of boiling water until *al dente*. Drain and return the pasta to the pan. Meanwhile, heat 2 teaspoons of the oil in a large frying pan. Add the sausages and cook, turning, for 5 minutes, or until well browned and cooked through. Drain on paper towels, then slice when they have cooled enough to touch. Keep warm.

2 Wipe clean the frying pan and heat the remaining oil. Add the onion and garlic and cook over medium heat for 2 minutes, or until the onion has softened. Add the tomato, sugar and 1 cup (250 ml/8½ fl oz) water and season well with ground black pepper. Reduce the heat and simmer for 12 minutes, or until thickened and reduced a little.

3 Pour the sauce over the cooked pasta and stir through the sausage, then the basil and half of the cheese. Divide among serving plates and serve hot with the remaining cheese sprinkled over the top.

ROASTED BUTTERNUT SAUCE ON PAPPARDELLE

Preparation time:
15 minutes

Cooking time:
35 minutes

Serves 4

INGREDIENTS

- 1.4 kg (3 lb 1 oz) butternut pumpkin (squash), cut into 2 cm (¾ inch) pieces
- 4 garlic cloves, crushed
- 3 teaspoons fresh thyme leaves
- 100 ml (3½ fl oz) olive oil
- 500 g (1 lb 2 oz) pappardelle
- 2 tablespoons cream
- ¾ cup (185 ml/6½ fl oz) hot chicken stock (broth)
- 30 g (1 oz) shaved Parmesan cheese

1 Preheat the oven to 200°C (400°F/Gas 6). Place the pumpkin (squash), garlic, thyme and ¼ cup (60 ml/2 fl oz) of the olive oil in a bowl and toss together. Season with salt, transfer to a baking tray (sheet) and cook for 30 minutes, or until tender and golden. Meanwhile, cook the pasta in a large saucepan of boiling water until *al dente*. Drain and return to the pan. Toss through the remaining oil and keep warm.

2 Place the cooked pumpkin (squash) and the cream in a food processor or blender and process until smooth. Add the hot stock (broth) and process until smooth and combined. Season with salt and ground black pepper and gently toss through the warm pasta. Divide among four serving plates, sprinkle with Parmesan and extra thyme leaves, if desired, and serve immediately.

NOTE: The sauce becomes gluggy on standing, so serve it as soon as possible.

SPINACH RAVIOLI WITH PINE NUT SALSA

Preparation time:
15 minutes

Cooking time:
10 minutes

Serves 4

INGREDIENTS

- 625 g (1 lb 6 oz) spinach ravioli
- 3½ tablespoons olive oil
- ⅓ cup (50 g / 1¼ oz) pine nuts
- 150 g (5¼ oz) semi-dried (sun-blushed) tomatoes, thinly sliced
- 270 g (9½ oz) jar roasted capsicums (peppers), drained and thinly sliced
- 2 tablespoons finely chopped fresh flat-leaf (Italian) parsley
- 2 tablespoons finely chopped fresh mint
- 1½ tablespoons balsamic vinegar
- 30 g (1 oz) shaved Parmesan cheese

1 Cook the pasta in a large saucepan of boiling water until *al dente*. Drain. Heat ½ teaspoon of the oil in a frying pan and gently cook the pine nuts until light gold. Remove from the pan and roughly chop.

2 Add the remaining oil to the pan and add the tomato, capsicum (pepper), parsley, mint and vinegar and stir until combined and warmed through. Remove from the heat and season to taste. Stir in the pine nuts. Divide the pasta among four serving plates, spoon on the sauce and top with the Parmesan. Serve immediately.

RICOTTA AND PASTA TIMBALES

Preparation time:
15 minutes

Cooking time:
45 minutes

Makes 4

INGREDIENTS

- ½ cup (125 ml/4¼ fl oz) light olive oil
- 1 large eggplant (aubergine), sliced lengthways into 1 cm (½ inch) slices
- 200 g (7 oz) straight macaroni
- 1 small onion, finely chopped
- 2 garlic cloves, crushed
- 400 g (14 oz) can chopped tomatoes
- 400 g (14 oz) ricotta cheese
- 1 cup (80 g/2¾ oz) coarsely grated Parmesan cheese
- ½ cup (15 g/½ oz) shredded fresh basil, plus extra to garnish

1 Preheat the oven to 180°C (350°F/Gas 4). Heat 2 tablespoons of the oil in a non-stick frying pan and cook the eggplant (aubergine) in three batches over medium heat for 2–3 minutes each side, or until golden, adding 2 tablespoons of the oil with each batch. Remove from the pan and drain on crumpled paper towels. Meanwhile, cook the pasta in a large saucepan of boiling water until *al dente*. Drain and set aside.

2 Add the onion and garlic to the frying pan and cook over medium heat for 2–3 minutes, or until just golden. Add the tomato and cook for 5 minutes, or until the sauce is pulpy and most of the liquid has evaporated. Season, then remove from the heat.

3 Combine the ricotta, Parmesan and basil, then mix in the pasta. Line the base and sides of four 1½ cup (375 ml/13 fl oz) ramekins with eggplant (aubergine), trimming any overhanging pieces. Top with half the pasta mix, pressing down firmly. Spoon on the tomato sauce, then cover with the remaining pasta Bake for 10–15 minutes, or until heated and golden on top. Stand for 5 minutes, then run a knife around the side to loosen the timbale. Invert onto plates, garnish with basil and serve with a side salad and bread.

CREAMY PASTA BAKE

Preparation time:
15 minutes

Cooking time:
40 minutes

Serves 4

INGREDIENTS

- 200 g (7 oz) risoni
- 40 g (1½ oz) butter
- 4 spring (green) onions, thinly sliced
- 400 g (14 oz) zucchini (courgettes), grated
- 4 eggs
- ½ cup (125 ml/4¼ fl oz) cream
- 100 g (3½ oz) ricotta cheese (see NOTE)
- ⅔ cup (100 g/3½ oz) grated mozzarella cheese
- ¾ cup (75 g/2⅔ oz) grated Parmesan cheese

1 Preheat the oven to 180°C (350°F/Gas 4). Cook the pasta in a large saucepan of boiling water until *al dente*. Drain well. Meanwhile, heat the butter in a frying pan, cook the spring (green) onion for 1 minute, then add the zucchini (courgette) and cook for a further 4 minutes, or until soft. Cool slightly.

2 Combine the eggs, cream, ricotta, mozzarella, risoni and half of the Parmesan well. Stir in the zucchini (courgette) mixture. Season. Spoon into four 2 cup (500 ml/17 fl oz) greased ovenproof dishes, but not to the brim. Sprinkle with the remaining Parmesan and cook for 25–30 minutes, or until firm and golden.

NOTE: With such simple flavours, it is important to use good-quality fresh ricotta from the delicatessen or the deli section of your local supermarket.

RICH CHEESE MACARONI

Preparation time:
15 minutes

Cooking time:
40 minutes

Serves 4

INGREDIENTS

- 450 g (15¾ oz) elbow macaroni
- 40 g (1½ oz) butter
- 300 ml (10 fl oz) cream
- 125 g (4⅓ oz) fontina cheese, sliced
- 125 g (4⅓ oz) provolone cheese, grated
- 100 g (3½ oz) Gruyère cheese, grated
- 125 g (4⅓ oz) blue castello cheese, crumbled
- ½ cup (40 g/1½ oz) fresh white breadcrumbs
- 25 g (¾ cup) grated Parmesan cheese

1 Preheat the oven to 180°C (350°F/Gas 4). Cook the pasta in a large saucepan of boiling water until *al dente*. Drain and keep warm. Melt half the butter in a large saucepan. Add the cream and, when just coming to the boil, add the fontina, provolone, Gruyère and blue castello cheeses, stirring constantly over low heat for 3 minutes, or until melted. Season with salt and ground white pepper. Add the pasta to the cheese mixture and mix well.

2 Spoon the mixture into a lightly greased shallow 8 cup (2 litre/2.1 US qt/1.75 UK qt) ovenproof dish. Sprinkle with the breadcrumbs mixed with the Parmesan, dot with the remaining cubed butter and bake for 25 minutes, or until the top is golden and crisp. Serve with a salad.

CREAMY TOMATO AND BACON PASTA

Preparation time:
10 minutes

Cooking time:
15 minutes

Serves 4

INGREDIENTS

- 400 g (14 oz) cresti di gallo
- 1 tablespoon olive oil
- 170 g (6 oz) streaky bacon, thinly sliced (see NOTE)
- 500 g (1 lb 2 oz) Roma (plum or egg-shaped) tomatoes, roughly chopped
- ½ cup (125 ml/4¼ fl oz) thick (double/heavy) cream
- 2 tablespoons sun-dried (sun-blushed) tomato pesto
- 2 tablespoons finely chopped fresh flat-leaf (Italian) parsley
- ½ cup (50 g/1¾ oz) finely grated Parmesan cheese

1 Cook the pasta in a large saucepan of boiling water until *al dente*. Drain and return to the pan. Meanwhile, heat the oil in a frying pan, add the bacon and cook over high heat for 2 minutes, or until starting to brown. Reduce the heat to medium, add the tomato and cook, stirring frequently, for 2 minutes, or until the tomato has softened but still holds its shape.

2 Stir in the cream and pesto until heated through. Remove from heat, add the parsley, then toss the sauce and Parmesan through the pasta.

NOTE: Streaky bacon is the tail end of bacon rashers. It is fattier but adds to the flavour of the meal. You can use 170 g (6 oz) bacon rashers if you prefer.

LINGUINE WITH HAM, ARTICHOKE AND LEMON SAUCE

Preparation time:
15 minutes

Cooking time:
10 minutes

Serves 4

INGREDIENTS

- 500 g (1 lb 2 oz) fresh linguine
- 25 g (¾ oz) butter
- 2 large garlic cloves, chopped
- 150 g (5¼ oz) marinated artichokes, drained and quartered
- 150 g (5¼ oz) sliced leg ham, cut into strips
- 300 ml (10 fl oz) cream
- 2 teaspoons coarsely grated lemon zest
- ½ cup (15 g/½ oz) fresh basil, torn
- ⅓ cup (35 g/1¼ oz) grated Parmesan cheese

1 Cook the pasta in a large saucepan of boiling water until *al dente*. Drain, then return to the pan. Meanwhile, melt the butter in a large frying pan, add the garlic and cook over medium heat for 1 minute, or until fragrant. Add the artichokes and ham and cook for a further 2 minutes.

2 Add the cream and lemon zest, reduce the heat and simmer for 5 minutes, gently breaking up the artichokes with a spoon. Pour the sauce over the pasta, then add the basil and Parmesan and toss until the pasta is evenly coated. Divide among four serving plates and serve.

FRESH FETTUCINE WITH SEARED TUNA

Preparation time:
15 minutes + 10 minutes marinating

Cooking time:
15 minutes

Serves 4–6

INGREDIENTS

- 4 × 200 g (7 oz) tuna steaks
- ⅔ cup (170 ml/5¾ fl oz) balsamic vinegar
- ½ cup (125 ml/4¼ fl oz) good-quality olive oil
- 1 lemon
- 1 garlic clove, finely chopped
- 1 red onion, finely chopped
- 2 tablespoons capers, rinsed and dried
- 10 g (⅓ cup) fresh flat-leaf (Italian) parsley, finely chopped
- 500 g (1 lb 2 oz) fresh fettucine

1 Place the tuna in a non-metallic dish and cover with the balsamic vinegar. Turn to coat evenly with the vinegar and marinate for 10 minutes. Heat 2 tablespoons of the oil in a large frying pan over medium heat and cook the tuna steaks for 2–3 minutes each side. Remove from the pan, cut into 2 cm (¾ inch) cubes and transfer to a bowl.

2 Finely grate the rind from the lemon to give ½ teaspoon zest, then squeeze the lemon to give ¼ cup (60 ml/2 fl oz) juice. Wipe the frying pan clean, and heat 2 tablespoons of the olive oil over medium heat, then add the garlic and cook for 30 seconds. Stir in the chopped onion and cook for 2 minutes. Add the lemon zest and capers and cook for 1 minute, then stir in the parsley and cook for 1 minute. Add the lemon juice and remaining oil and gently toss together. Season to taste.

3 Meanwhile, cook the pasta in a large saucepan of boiling water until *al dente*. Drain well, return to the pan and toss the caper mixture through. Divide the pasta among serving bowls and arrange the tuna pieces over the top.

GARLIC AND CHILLI OIL SPAGHETTI

Preparation time:
15 minutes

Cooking time:
15 minutes

Serves 4–6

INGREDIENTS

- 1 cup (250 ml/8½ fl oz) good-quality olive oil
- 2 bird's eye chillies, seeded and thinly sliced
- 5–6 large cloves garlic, crushed
- 500 g (1 lb 2 oz) spaghetti
- 100 g (3½ oz) thinly sliced prosciutto
- ½ cup (30 g/1 oz) chopped fresh flat-leaf (Italian) parsley
- 2 tablespoons chopped fresh basil
- 2 tablespoons chopped fresh oregano
- ¾ cup (75 g/2⅔ oz) good-quality grated Parmesan cheese

1 Pour the oil into a small saucepan with the chilli and garlic. Slowly heat the oil over low heat for about 12 minutes to infuse the oil with the garlic and chilli. Don't allow the oil to reach smoking point or the garlic will burn and taste bitter.

2 Meanwhile, cook the pasta in a large saucepan of boiling water until *al dente*. Drain well and return to the pan. Lay the prosciutto on a grill (broiler) tray and cook under a hot grill (broiler) for 2 minutes each side, or until crispy. Cool and break into pieces.

3 Pour the hot oil mixture over the spaghetti and toss well with the prosciutto, fresh herbs and Parmesan. Season to taste.

NOTE: This is a very simple dish, but it relies on good-quality ingredients.

ANGEL HAIR PASTA WITH SCALLOPS

Preparation time:
15 minutes

Cooking time:
15 minutes

Serves 4

INGREDIENTS

- 350 g (12¼ oz) angel hair pasta
- 100 g (3½ oz) butter
- 3 garlic cloves, crushed
- 24 scallops, without roe
- 150 g (5¼ oz) baby rocket (arugula) leaves
- 2 teaspoons finely grated lemon zest
- ¼ cup (60 ml/2 fl oz) lemon juice
- 125 g (4⅓ oz) semi-dried (sun-blushed) tomatoes, thinly sliced
- 30 g (1 oz) shaved Parmesan cheese

1 Cook the pasta in a large saucepan of boiling water until *al dente*. Meanwhile, melt the butter in a small saucepan, add the garlic and cook over low heat, stirring, for 1 minute. Remove from the heat.

2 Heat a lightly greased chargrill (charbroil) plate over high heat and cook the scallops, brushing occasionally with some of the garlic butter for 1–2 minutes each side, or until cooked. Set aside and keep warm.

3 Drain the pasta and return to the pan with the remaining garlic butter, the rocket (arugula), lemon zest, lemon juice and tomato and toss until combined. Divide among four serving plates and top with the scallops. Season to taste and sprinkle with Parmesan.

SPAGHETTI MARINARA

Preparation time:
15 minutes

Cooking time:
35 minutes

Serves 4–6

INGREDIENTS

- 2 tablespoons olive oil
- 1 onion, finely chopped
- 2 garlic cloves, crushed
- 2 × 400 g (14 oz) cans
  chopped tomatoes
- ¼ cup (60 g/2 oz) tomato paste
  (tomato puree)
- 500 g (1 lb 2 oz) spaghetti
- 500 g (1 lb 2 oz) good-quality
  marinara mix (see NOTE)
- 8 black mussels, beards
  removed, scrubbed
- 2 tablespoons shredded fresh basil

1 Heat the oil in a saucepan over
  medium heat, add the onion and
  cook for 5 minutes, or until
  softened and lightly browned.
  Add the garlic and stir for
  another 1 minute, or until
  aromatic. Add the tomato and
  tomato paste (tomato puree)
  and bring to the boil, then
  reduce the heat and simmer for
  20–25 minutes, or until the sauce
  becomes rich and pulpy. Stir the
  sauce occasionally during
  cooking. Season with salt and
  ground black pepper. Meanwhile,
  cook the pasta in a large saucepan
  of boiling water until *al dente*.
  Drain well, return to the
  saucepan and keep warm.

2 Add the marinara mix and the
  mussels to the tomato sauce and
  cook for about 2–3 minutes, or
  until the seafood is cooked and
  the mussels are open. Discard any
  mussels that do not open. Stir in
  the basil. Toss the sauce through
  the warm pasta and serve.

NOTE: Marinara mix is available
from seafood stores. Try to choose a
good-quality marinara mix to avoid
chewy seafood. Alternatively, you
can make your own by choosing a
few different types of seafood, such
as octopus, fish fillets and calamari,
and chopping into bite-size pieces.

SPAGHETTI PRIMAVERA

Preparation time:
15 minutes

Cooking time:
15 minutes

Serves 4

INGREDIENTS

- 400 g (14 oz) spaghetti
- ⅓ cup (80 ml/2¾ fl oz) extra virgin olive oil
- 200 g (7 oz) fresh asparagus, trimmed and cut into 5 cm (2 inch) lengths
- 1 cup (155 g/5½ oz) frozen peas
- 1 cup (155 g/5½ oz) frozen broad (fava) beans
- 1 leek, thinly sliced
- 2 tablespoons finely chopped fresh flat-leaf (Italian) parsley
- 1 cup (250 ml/8½ fl oz) thick (double/heavy) cream
- ⅓ cup (35 g/1¼ oz) grated Parmesan cheese

1 Cook the pasta in a large saucepan of boiling water until *al dente*. Rinse and drain well, then return to the pan, toss with 2 tablespoons of the oil and keep warm.

2 Meanwhile, bring a saucepan of water to the boil and cook the asparagus and peas for 2 minutes, or until bright green and tender. Remove with a slotted spoon and plunge into cold water. Return the pan to the boil and cook the broad (fava) beans for 2 minutes, or until tender. Drain, cool, then slip off their skins.

3 Heat the remaining oil in a frying pan and cook the leek over low heat for 2–3 minutes, or until soft but not brown. Add the blanched vegetables and cook for 1 minute, or until warmed through. Stir in the parsley and cream and simmer for 2–3 minutes. Toss the sauce and Parmesan through the pasta, season well and serve.

NOTE: If fresh broad (fava) beans and peas are in season, use them and peel the pods before cooking.

SMOKED CHICKEN LINGUINE

Preparation time:
15 minutes

Cooking time:
20 minutes

Serves 4

INGREDIENTS

- 1 tablespoon olive oil
- 1 leek, thinly sliced
- 3 large garlic cloves, finely chopped
- ½ cup (125 ml/4¼ fl oz) dry white wine
- 300 g (10½ oz) Swiss brown mushrooms, sliced
- 2 teaspoons chopped fresh thyme
- 300 ml (10 fl oz) thick (double/heavy) cream
- 2 smoked chicken breast fillets, thinly sliced (see NOTE)
- 350 g (12¼ oz) fresh linguine

1 Heat the oil in a saucepan. Add the leek and cook, stirring, over low heat for 3–4 minutes, or until soft. Add the garlic and cook for another minute. Pour in the wine and simmer for 2–3 minutes, or until the liquid has reduced by half.

2 Increase the heat to medium, add the mushrooms and thyme and cook for 5 minutes, or until any excess liquid has been absorbed, then add the cream and sliced chicken. Reduce the heat and simmer for 4–5 minutes, or until the sauce has slightly thickened. Meanwhile, cook the pasta in a large saucepan of boiling water until *al dente*. Drain and divide among serving plates. Spoon on the sauce and serve.

NOTE: You can buy smoked chicken at the deli section of some supermarkets and good delicatessens.

FETTUCINE WITH SPINACH AND ROAST TOMATO

Preparation time:
10 minutes

Cooking time:
35 minutes

Serves 4–6

INGREDIENTS

- 6 Roma (plum or egg-shaped) tomatoes
- 40 g (1½ oz) butter
- 2 garlic cloves, crushed
- 1 onion, chopped
- 500 g (1 lb 2 oz) English (common) spinach, trimmed
- 1 cup (250 ml/8½ fl oz) vegetable stock (broth)
- ½ cup (125 ml/4¼ fl oz) thick (double/heavy) cream
- 500 g (1 lb 2 oz) fresh spinach fettucine
- 50 g (1¾ oz) shaved Parmesan cheese

1 Preheat the oven to 220°C (425°F/Gas 7). Cut the tomatoes in half lengthways, then cut each half into three wedges. Place the wedges on a lightly greased baking tray (sheet) and bake for 30–35 minutes, or until softened and slightly golden. Meanwhile, heat the butter in a large frying pan. Add the garlic and onion and cook over medium heat for 5 minutes, or until the onion is soft. Add the spinach, stock (broth) and cream, increase the heat to high and bring to the boil. Simmer rapidly for 5 minutes.

2 While the spinach mixture is cooking, cook the pasta in a large saucepan of boiling water until *al dente*. Drain and return to the pan. Remove the spinach from the heat and season well. Cool slightly, then process in a food processor until smooth. Toss through the pasta until well coated. Divide among serving bowls, top with the roasted tomatoes and Parmesan shavings.

RAVIOLI IN ROASTED VEGETABLE SAUCE

Preparation time:
15 minutes

Cooking time:
15 minutes

Serves 4

INGREDIENTS

- 6 red capsicums (peppers)
- 6 slices prosciutto
- 625 g (1 lb 6 oz) chicken or ricotta ravioli
- 2 tablespoons olive oil
- 3 garlic cloves, crushed
- 2 leeks, thinly sliced
- 1 tablespoon chopped fresh oregano
- 2 teaspoons soft brown sugar
- 1 cup (250 ml / 8½ fl oz) hot chicken stock (broth)

1 Cut the capsicums (peppers) into large pieces, removing the seeds and membrane. Place, skin-side-up, under a hot grill (broiler) until the skin blackens and blisters. Cool in a plastic bag, then peel away the skin.

Place the prosciutto under the grill (broiler) and cook for 1 minute each side, or until crisp. Break into pieces and set aside.

2 Cook the pasta in a large saucepan of boiling water until *al dente*. Meanwhile, heat the oil in a frying pan and cook the garlic and leek over medium heat for 3–4 minutes, or until softened. Add the oregano and sugar and stir for 1 minute.

3 Place the capsicum (pepper) and leek mixture in a food processor or blender, season with salt and pepper and process until combined. Add the chicken stock (broth) and process until smooth. Drain the pasta and return to the saucepan. Gently toss the sauce through the ravioli over low heat until warmed through. Divide among four serving bowls and sprinkle with prosciutto.

AGNOLOTTI WITH ALFREDO SAUCE

Preparation time:
10 minutes

Cooking time:
10 minutes

Serves 4–6

INGREDIENTS

- 625 g (1 lb 6 oz) agnolotti
- 90 g (3¼ oz) butter
- 1½ cups (150 g/5¼ oz) grated Parmesan cheese
- 300 ml (10 fl oz) cream
- 2 tablespoons chopped fresh marjoram

1 Cook the pasta in a large saucepan of boiling water until *al dente*. Drain and return to the pan.

2 Just before the pasta is cooked, melt the butter in a saucepan over low heat. Add the Parmesan and cream and bring to the boil. Reduce the heat and simmer, stirring constantly, for 2 minutes, or until the sauce has thickened slightly. Stir in the marjoram and season with salt and ground black pepper. Toss the sauce through the pasta until well coated and serve immediately.

VARIATION: Marjoram can be replaced with any other fresh herb you prefer – for example, try parsley, thyme, chervil or dill (dill weed).

SPAGHETTI NICOISE

Preparation time:
10 minutes

Cooking time:
15 minutes

Serves 4–6

INGREDIENTS

- 350 g (12¼ oz) spaghetti
- 8 quail eggs (or 4 hen eggs)
- 1 lemon
- 3 × 185 g (6½ oz) cans good-quality tuna in oil
- ⅓ cup (50 g/1¾ oz) pitted and halved Kalamata olives
- 100 g (3½ oz) semi-dried (sun-blushed) tomatoes, cut lengthways
- 4 anchovy fillets, chopped into small pieces
- 3 tablespoons baby capers, drained
- 3 tablespoons chopped fresh flat-leaf (Italian) parsley

1 Cook the pasta in a large saucepan of boiling water until *al dente*. Meanwhile, place the eggs in a saucepan of cold water, bring to the boil and cook for 4 minutes (10 minutes for hen eggs). Drain, cool under cold water, then peel. Cut the quail eggs into halves or the hen eggs into quarters. Finely grate the rind of the lemon to give 1 teaspoon of grated zest. Then, squeeze the lemon to give 2 tablespoons juice.

2 Empty the tuna and its oil into a large bowl. Add the olives, tomato halves, anchovies, lemon zest and juice, capers and 2 tablespoons of the parsley. Drain the pasta and rinse in a little cold water, then toss gently through the tuna mixture. Divide among serving bowls, garnish with egg and the extra chopped fresh parsley, and serve.

TORTELLINI WITH MUSHROOM SAUCE

Preparation time:
15 minutes

Cooking time:
20 minutes

Serves 4

INGREDIENTS

- 500 g (1 lb 2 oz) tortellini
- ¼ cup (60 ml/2 fl oz) olive oil
- 600 g (1 lb 5 oz) Swiss brown mushrooms, thinly sliced
- 2 garlic cloves, crushed
- ½ cup (125 ml/4¼ fl oz) dry white wine
- 300 ml (10 fl oz) thick (double/heavy) cream
- pinch ground nutmeg
- 3 tablespoons finely chopped fresh flat-leaf (Italian) parsley
- 30 g (1 oz) grated Parmesan cheese

1 Cook the pasta in a large saucepan of boiling water until *al dente*. Drain. Meanwhile, heat the oil in a frying pan over medium heat. Add the mushrooms and cook, stirring occasionally, for 5 minutes, or until softened. Add the garlic and cook for 1 minute, then stir in the wine and cook for 5 minutes, or until the liquid has reduced by half.

2 Add the cream, nutmeg and parsley, stir to combine and cook for 3–5 minutes, or until it thickens slightly. Season. Divide the tortellini among four bowls and spoon on the sauce and sprinkle with Parmesan.

PROSCIUTTO AND SPINACH LASAGNE

Preparation time:
15 minutes + 10 minutes standing

Cooking time:
25 minutes

Serves 4–6

INGREDIENTS

- 600 g (1 lb 5 oz) bottled tomato pasta (marinara) sauce
- 250 g (8¾ oz) fresh lasagne sheets
- 400 g (14 oz) bocconcini, thinly sliced
- 500 g (1 lb 2 oz) English (common) spinach, trimmed
- ½ cup (125 ml/4¼ fl oz) cream
- 10 thin slices prosciutto, chopped
- 1 cup (150 g/5¼ oz) grated mozzarella cheese
- ½ cup (50 g/1¾ oz) finely grated Parmesan cheese

1 Preheat the oven to 180°C (350°F/Gas 4). Lightly grease a 12 cup (3 litre/3.2 US qt/ 2.6 UK qt) shallow 23 cm × 30 cm (9 × 12 inch) ovenproof dish. Spread half of the tomato pasta (marinara) sauce over the base of the dish. Cover the layer of pasta sauce with a third of the lasagne sheets. Top with half of the bocconcini and half of the spinach. Drizzle on half of the cream and sprinkle with half of the prosciutto. Season with some salt and ground black pepper. Repeat to give two layers, starting with half of the remaining lasagne sheets.

2 Lay the final layer of lasagne over the top and spread with the remaining pasta sauce. Sprinkle with the combined mozzarella and Parmesan. Bake for 25 minutes, or until cooked. Leave to stand for 10 minutes before serving.

MUSHROOM AND RICOTTA CANNELLONI

Preparation time:
15 minutes

Cooking time:
30 minutes

Serves 4

INGREDIENTS

- 500 g (1 lb 2 oz) button mushrooms
- 200 g (7 oz) fresh lasagne sheets
- 2 tablespoons olive oil
- 3 garlic cloves, crushed
- 2 tablespoons lemon juice
- 400 g (14 oz) fresh ricotta cheese
- 3 tablespoons chopped fresh basil
- 425 g (15 oz) bottled tomato pasta (marinara) sauce
- 1 cup (150 g/5¼ oz) grated mozzarella cheese

1 Preheat the oven to 180°C (350°F/Gas 4). Place the mushrooms in a food processor and pulse until finely chopped. Cut the lasagne sheets into twelve 13 × 16 cm (5 × 6⅓ inch) rectangles.

2 Heat the oil in a large frying pan over medium heat. Add the garlic and mushrooms and cook, stirring, for 3 minutes. Add the lemon juice and cook for 2 minutes, or until softened. Transfer to a sieve over a bowl to collect the juices, pressing with a spoon to remove as much moisture as possible. Reserve.

3 Combine the mushrooms, ricotta and basil. Season well. Place heaped tablespoons of the mixture along one long edge of the lasagne sheet. Roll up, then place in a greased 8 cup (2 litre/2.1 US qt/1.75 UK qt) 16 × 30 cm (6⅓ × 12 inch) ovenproof ceramic dish. Repeat with the remaining mixture and sheets, placing them in a single layer. Pour on the reserved mushroom cooking liquid, then pour on the pasta sauce. Sprinkle with cheese and bake for 25 minutes, or until golden and bubbling. Serve with salad.

PRAWN SAFFRON RISOTTO

Preparation time:
20 minutes

Total cooking time:
40 minutes

Serves 4

INGREDIENTS

- ¼ teaspoon saffron threads
- 500 g (1 lb 2 oz) raw prawns (shrimp)
- ⅓ cup (80 ml/2¾ fl oz) olive oil
- 2 cloves garlic, crushed
- 3 tablespoons chopped parsley
- 3 tablespoons dry sherry
- 3 tablespoons white wine
- 6 cups (1.5 litres/1.6 US qt/ 1.3 UK qt) fish stock (broth)
- 1 onion, diced
- 2 cups (440 g/15½ oz) arborio rice

1 Soak the saffron threads in 3 tablespoons water. Peel the prawns (shrimp) and devein, leaving the tails intact. Heat 2 tablespoons of the olive oil in a pan. Add the garlic, parsley and prawns (shrimp) and season with salt and pepper, to taste. Cook for 2 minutes, then add the sherry, wine and saffron threads with their liquid. Remove the prawns (shrimp) with a slotted spoon. Simmer until the liquid has reduced by half. Add the fish stock (broth) and 1 cup (250 ml/8½ fl oz) water and leave to simmer.

2 In a separate large, heavy-based pan heat the remaining oil. Add the onion and rice and cook for 3 minutes. Keeping the pan of stock (broth) constantly at simmering point, add ½ cup (125 ml/4¼ oz) hot stock (broth) to the rice mixture. Stir constantly over low heat, with a wooden spoon, until all the liquid has been absorbed. Add another half cupful of stock (broth) and repeat the process until all the stock (broth) has been added and the rice is tender and creamy — this will take 25–30 minutes.

3 Stir in the prawns (shrimp), warm through and serve, perhaps with freshly grated Parmesan cheese.

NOTE: Saffron is the most expensive spice in the world but only a very tiny amount is necessary.

MUSHROOM AND PANCETTA RISOTTO

Preparation time:
15 minutes

Cooking time:
35 minutes

Serves 4–6

INGREDIENTS

- 25 g (¾ oz) butter
- 2 garlic cloves, finely chopped
- 150 g (5¼ oz) piece pancetta, diced
- 400 g (14 oz) button mushrooms, sliced
- 500 g (1 lb 2 oz) risoni
- 1 litre (1.1 US qt/1.75 UK qt) chicken stock (broth)
- 125 ml (4¼ fl oz) cream
- 50 g (1¾ oz) finely grated Parmesan cheese
- 4 tablespoons finely chopped fresh flat-leaf (Italian) parsley

1 Melt the butter in a saucepan, add the garlic and cook over medium heat for 30 seconds, then increase the heat to high, add the pancetta and cook for 3–5 minutes, or until crisp. Add the mushrooms and cook for 3–5 minutes, or until softened.

2 Add the risoni, stir until coated in the mixture. Add the stock (broth) and bring to the boil. Reduce the heat to medium and cook, covered, for 15–20 minutes, or until nearly all the liquid has evaporated and the risoni is tender.

3 Stir in the cream and cook, uncovered, for a further 3 minutes, stirring occasionally until the cream is absorbed. Stir in ⅓ cup (35g/1¼ oz) of the Parmesan and all the parsley and season to taste. Divide among four serving bowls and serve sprinkled with the remaining Parmesan.

PEA AND PANCETTA RISOTTO

Preparation time:
25 minutes

Total cooking time:
45 minutes

Serves 4

INGREDIENTS

- 1 tablespoon olive oil
- 1 celery stick (rib), chopped
- 2 tablespoons chopped fresh flat-leaf parsley
- freshly ground black pepper
- 75 g (2⅔ oz) sliced pancetta, coarsely chopped
- 250 g (8¾ oz) peas (fresh or frozen)
- ½ cup (125 ml/4¼ fl oz) dry white wine
- 3 cups (750 ml/26 fl oz) chicken stock (broth)
- 60 g (2 oz) butter
- 1 onion, chopped
- 2 cups (440 g/15½ oz) arborio rice
- ⅓ cup (35 g/1¼ oz) freshly grated Parmesan

1 Heat the oil in a frying pan, add the celery, parsley and black pepper and cook over medium heat for a few minutes to soften the celery. Add the pancetta and stir until it just begins to curl. Add the peas and half the wine, bring to the boil, then reduce the heat and simmer uncovered until almost all the liquid has evaporated. Set aside.

2 Put the stock (broth) and 3 cups (750 ml/26 fl oz) water in a separate pan and keep at simmering point.

3 Heat the butter in a large heavy-based saucepan. Add the onion and stir until softened. Add the rice and stir well. Pour in the remaining wine; allow it to bubble and evaporate. Add ½ cup (125 ml/4¼ oz) hot stock (broth) to the rice mixture. Stir constantly over low heat, with a wooden spoon, until all the stock (broth) has been absorbed. Repeat the process until all the stock (broth) has been added and the rice is creamy and tender (about 25–30 minutes).

4 Add the pea mixture and
Parmesan and serve immediately.
Serve with Parmesan shavings and
black pepper.

NOTE: If fresh peas are in season,
500 g (1 lb 2 oz) peas in the pod
will yield about 250 g (8¾ oz)
shelled peas.

CARROT AND PUMPKIN RISOTTO

Preparation time:
15 minutes

Total cooking time:
35 minutes

Serves 4

INGREDIENTS

- 90 g (3¼ oz) butter
- 1 onion, finely chopped
- 250 g (8¾ oz) pumpkin, peeled and cut into small cubes
- 2 carrots, cut into small cubes
- 7–8 cups (1.75–2 litres; 1.8 US qt/ 1.5 UK qt–2.1 US qt/1.8 UK qt) vegetable stock (broth)
- 2 cups (440 g/15½ oz) arborio rice
- 90 g (3¼ oz) freshly grated Romano cheese
- ¼ teaspoon nutmeg
- freshly ground black pepper

1 Heat 60 g (2 oz) of the butter in a large, heavy-based pan. Add the onion and fry for 1–2 minutes, or until soft. Add the pumpkin and carrot and cook for 6–8 minutes, or until tender. Mash slightly with a potato masher. In a separate saucepan keep the stock (broth) at simmering point.

2 Add the rice to the vegetables and cook for 1 minute, stirring constantly. Ladle in enough hot stock (broth) to cover the rice; stir well. Reduce the heat and add more stock (broth) as it is absorbed, stirring frequently. Continue until the rice is tender and creamy (about 25 minutes).

3 Remove from the heat, add the remaining butter, cheese, nutmeg and pepper and fork through. Cover and leave for 5 minutes before serving.

NOTE: Romano is a hard, grating cheese similar to Parmesan.

BAKED POLENTA
WITH THREE CHEESES

Preparation time:
20 minutes + 2 hours chilling

Total cooking time:
45 minutes

Serves 4

INGREDIENTS

POLENTA
- 2½ cups (600 ml/20 fl oz) chicken stock (broth)
- 2 cups (300 g/10½ oz) polenta (cornmeal)
- ½ cup (50 g/1¾ oz) freshly grated Parmesan

CHEESE FILLING
- 100 g (3½ oz) havarti cheese, sliced
- 100 g (3½ oz) mascarpone
- 100 g (3½ oz) blue cheese, crumbled
- 100 g (3½ oz) butter, sliced thinly
- ½ cup (50 g/1¾ oz) freshly grated Parmesan

1 **To make Polenta:** Brush a 7-cup (1.75 litre/1.8 US qt/1.5 UK qt) loaf tin with oil. Put the stock (broth) and 2 cups (500 ml/17 fl oz) water in a large pan and bring to the boil. Add the polenta (cornmeal) and stir for 10 minutes until very thick.

2 Remove from the heat and stir in the Parmesan. Spread into the tin and smooth the surface. Refrigerate for 2 hours, then cut into about 30 thin slices. Preheat the oven to moderate 180°C (350°F/Gas 4).

3 Brush a large ovenproof dish with oil. Place a layer of polenta slices on the base. Top with a layer of half the combined havarti, mascarpone and blue cheeses and half the butter. Add another layer of polenta and top with the remainder of the three cheeses and butter. Add a final layer of polenta and sprinkle the Parmesan on top. Bake for 30 minutes, or until a golden crust forms. Serve immediately.

NOTE: Polenta is available from most supermarkets and delicatessens.

NOTE: Havarti is actually a Danish cheese with a full flavour.

POLENTA WITH WILD MUSHROOMS

Preparation time:
30 minutes + chilling

Total cooking time:
1 hour 20 minutes

Serves 6–8

INGREDIENTS

POLENTA
- 2½ cups (600 ml/20 fl oz) chicken stock (broth)
- 2 cups (300 g/10½ oz) polenta (cornmeal)
- 1 cup (100 g/3½ oz) freshly grated Parmesan

MUSHROOM SAUCE
- 1 kg (2 lb 3 oz) mixed mushrooms (roman, oyster and flat)
- ½ cup (125 ml/4¼ fl oz) olive oil
- ½ cup (15 g/½ oz) chopped parsley
- 4 cloves garlic, finely chopped
- 1 onion, chopped

1 **To make Polenta:** Put the stock (broth) and 2 cups (500 ml/ 17 fl oz) water in a large pan and bring to the boil. Add the polenta (cornmeal) and stir constantly for 10 minutes until very thick. Remove from the heat and stir in the Parmesan. Brush a 20 cm (8 inch) round spring-form tin with oil. Spread the polenta mixture into the tin and smooth the surface. Refrigerate for 2 hours, turn out and cut into 6–8 wedges.

2 **To make Mushroom Sauce:** Wipe the mushrooms with a damp cloth and roughly chop the larger ones. Put the mushrooms, oil, parsley, garlic and onion in a pan. Stir, cover and leave to simmer for 50 minutes, or until cooked through. Uncover and cook for 10 minutes, or until there is very little liquid left. Set aside.

3 Brush one side of the polenta with olive oil and cook under a preheated grill (broiler) for 5 minutes, or until the edges are browned. Turn over and brown. Reheat the Mushroom Sauce and serve spooned over slices of polenta.

NOTE: Use just button mushrooms if the other varieties aren't available.

CARAWAY POLENTA WITH LEEKS

Preparation time:
10 minutes

Total cooking time:
30 minutes

Serves 4

INGREDIENTS

- 6 cups (1.5 litres/1.6 US qt/
  1.3 UK qt) chicken stock (broth)
- 1½ cups (225 g/8 oz)
  polenta (cornmeal)
- 2 teaspoons caraway seeds
- 45 g (1⅔ oz) butter
- 2 large leeks, cut into thin strips
- 250 g (8¾ oz) Italian Fontina
  cheese, cut into cubes

1 Place the stock (broth) in a
large heavy-based pan and bring
to the boil. Pour in the polenta
(cornmeal) in a fine stream,
stirring continuously. Add the
caraway seeds and then reduce
the heat and simmer for about
20–25 minutes, or until the
polenta (cornmeal) is very soft.

2 Melt the butter in a frying pan
over moderate heat and add the
leeks. Cover and cook gently,
stirring occasionally, until wilted.
Add the Fontina cubes, stir a
couple of times and remove
from the heat.

3 Pour the polenta onto individual
plates in nest shapes and spoon
the leeks and cheese into
the centre.

HINT: Ready-made stock (broth)
can be quite salty, so use half stock
(broth), half water.

NOTE: Polenta is available from
most supermarkets and delicatessens.

OVEN-BAKED POTATO, LEEK AND OLIVES

Preparation time:
20 minutes

Total cooking time:
1 hour

Serves 4–6

INGREDIENTS

- 2 tablespoons extra virgin olive oil
- 1 leek, finely sliced
- 1½ cups (375 ml/13 fl oz) chicken stock (broth)
- 2 teaspoons chopped fresh thyme
- 1 kg (2 lb 3 oz) potatoes, unpeeled, cut into thin slices
- 6–8 pitted black (ripe) olives, sliced
- ½ cup (50 g/1¾ oz) freshly grated Parmesan
- 30 g (1 oz) butter, chopped

1 Preheat the oven to moderate 180°C (350°F/Gas 4). Brush a shallow 5-cup (1.25 litre/1.3 US qt/1.1 UK qt) ovenproof dish with a little olive oil. Heat the remaining oil in a large pan and cook the leek over moderate heat until soft. Add the stock (broth), thyme and potato. Cover and leave to simmer for 5 minutes.

2 Using tongs, lift out half the potato and put in the ovenproof dish. Sprinkle with olives and Parmesan, and season with salt and pepper.

3 Layer with the remaining potato, then spoon the leek and stock (broth) mixture in at the side of the dish, keeping the top dry.

4 Scatter chopped butter over the potato and then bake, uncovered, for 50 minutes, or until cooked and golden brown. Leave in a warm place for about 10 minutes before serving.

NOTE: Keeping the top layer of potato dry as you pour in the stock (broth) mixture will give it a crisp finish.

OLIVE AND LEMON LAMB CUTLETS

Preparation time:
15 minutes + marinating

Total cooking time:
10 minutes

Serves 4

INGREDIENTS

- 12 lamb cutlets
- 2 tablespoons olive oil
- juice and zest of 1 lemon
- 1 clove garlic, crushed
- 1 teaspoon finely chopped fresh
  rosemary leaves
- 1 teaspoon butter
- 16 black (ripe) olives, cut into strips
- 2 tablespoons chopped parsley

1 Trim the lamb cutlets of fat and place in a dish. Pour over 1 tablespoon of the oil, the lemon juice and zest, garlic and chopped rosemary. Leave to marinate for at least 30 minutes.

2 Heat the remaining oil and the butter in a large frying pan. Drain the cutlets, reserving the marinade, and fry over medium heat until cooked through, turning once. Remove from the pan and set aside.

3 Drain the excess fat from the pan and add the olives, parsley and remaining marinade. Bring to the boil and cook for 2 minutes. Season to taste with salt and pepper, pour over the cutlets and serve with mashed or roasted potatoes.

PORK SCALOPPINI
WITH LEMON SAUCE

Preparation time:
5 minutes

Total cooking time:
5 minutes

Serves 4

INGREDIENTS

- 3 tablespoons olive oil
- 60 g (2 oz) butter
- 8 thin pork steaks
- plain (all-purpose) flour, for coating
- 2 tablespoons lemon juice
- 2 tablespoons finely chopped parsley
- lemon slices, to garnish

1 Heat the oil and half the butter in a large frying pan until quite hot. Coat the pork in the flour and add to the pan, cooking in batches if necessary. Cook until lightly browned on one side, then turn over and brown the other side. Transfer to a warm plate and season with salt and pepper.

2 Lower the heat and add the lemon juice, parsley and remaining butter to the pan, stirring to combine. Add the pork steaks, turning them in the sauce.

3 Serve the pork steaks with the sauce. Garnish with lemon slices.

NOTE: For thin pork steaks, cover them with plastic wrap and beat with a rolling pin or meat mallet.

TUNA STEAKS WITH WARM BEAN SALAD

Preparation time:
15 minutes

Total cooking time:
10 minutes

Serves 4

INGREDIENTS

- 4 tuna steaks
- olive oil, for brushing
- finely shredded rind of 1 lemon

WARM BEAN SALAD
- 3 tablespoons olive oil
- 1 clove garlic, crushed
- 3 spring (green) onions, chopped
- 1 small red capsicum (pepper), chopped
- 600 g (1 lb 5 oz) can cannellini (white kidney) beans, rinsed and drained
- 1 radicchio (red chicory), washed and separated into leaves
- 12 small black (ripe) olives
- 1 tablespoon lemon juice

1 Brush the tuna steaks with oil and cook in a frying pan (or ribbed pan or char-grill/char-broiler) for 2–3 minutes each side. (Tuna should be rare in the centre but you may prefer to cook it for another minute each side.) Transfer to a plate, cover loosely with foil and leave in a warm place for 5 minutes.

2 **To make Warm Bean Salad:** Heat the oil in a pan and cook the garlic, spring (green) onions and capsicum (pepper) until soft but not brown. Add the beans and radicchio (red chicory) and stir gently until the radicchio is wilted. Add the olives and lemon juice and season to taste with salt and pepper.

3 Place the salad on individual plates, top with the tuna steaks and lemon rind. Serve immediately.

HINT: Use a lemon zester to make fine shreds of lemon rind.

SPRING CHICKEN WITH HONEY GLAZE

Preparation time:
15 minutes

Total cooking time:
55 minutes

Serves 6–8

INGREDIENTS

- 2 small (1.5 kg/3 lb 5 oz) chickens
- 1 tablespoon light olive oil

HONEY GLAZE
- 3 tablespoons honey
- juice and finely grated rind of 1 lemon
- 1 tablespoon finely chopped rosemary
- 1 tablespoon dry white wine
- 1 tablespoon white wine vinegar
- 2 teaspoons Dijon mustard
- 1½ tablespoons olive oil

1 Preheat the oven to moderate 180°C (350°F/Gas 4). Halve the chickens by cutting down either side of the backbone. Discard the backbones. Cut the chickens into quarters; brush with oil and season lightly. Place on a rack in a roasting pan, skin-side-down, and roast for 20 minutes.

2 **To make Honey Glaze:** Combine all the ingredients in a small pan. Bring to the boil, reduce the heat and simmer for 5 minutes.

3 After cooking one side, turn the chickens over and baste well with the warm glaze. Return to the oven and roast for 20 minutes. Baste once more and cook for a further 15 minutes. Serve hot or cold.

NOTE: To test if the chicken is cooked, pierce the meat at its thickest point. The juices should run clear.

STUFFED CALAMARI

Preparation time:
30 minutes

Total cooking time:
20 minutes

Serves 4

INGREDIENTS

- 8 medium calamari tubes
- 40 g (1½ oz) butter
- 8 slices pancetta, finely chopped
- 400 g (14 oz) raw prawns (shrimp), peeled, deveined and finely chopped
- 1 cup (80 g/2¾ oz) fresh breadcrumbs
- ¼ cup (10 g/⅓ oz) chopped fresh parsley
- 1 cup (100 g/3½ oz) grated Parmesan
- 100 g (3½ oz) butter, extra
- 3 cloves garlic, crushed
- 1 tablespoon chopped fresh parsley, extra

1 Rinse the calamari under cold water. Put your hand in and remove the insides and quill. Then remove the purple skin from the outside. Rinse and pat dry with paper towels.

2 Melt the butter in a small frying pan; cook the pancetta and prawns (shrimp) over high heat until the prawns (shrimp) are just cooked. Transfer to a bowl; add the breadcrumbs, parsley and Parmesan and mix well.

3 Divide the filling among the calamari tubes. Melt the extra butter with the garlic in a large frying pan and cook the stuffed calamari, in batches, for 3–4 minutes on each side, or until just cooked. Stir through the extra parsley. Place two stuffed calamari on each plate and spoon over a little of the garlic butter.

NOTE: You will only need to three-quarters-fill each calamari tube – the tubes shrink a little when cooked and if there is too much filling it will ooze out from the top.

MUSSELS IN TWO SAUCES

Preparation time:
25 minutes

Total cooking time:
45 minutes

Serves 4

INGREDIENTS

- 3 tablespoons olive oil
- 1.25 kg (2 lb 12 oz) mussels in shells, scrubbed
- 3 tablespoons grated mozzarella
- 2 tablespoons grated Parmesan

TOMATO SAUCE
- 2 cloves garlic, crushed
- ½ cup (125 ml/4¼ fl oz) white wine
- 3 tablespoons tomato paste (tomato puree)

WHITE SAUCE
- 25 g (¾ oz) butter
- ¼ cup (30 g/1 oz) plain (all-purpose) flour
- 1 cup (250 ml/8½ fl oz) milk

1 Heat half the oil in a large pan. Add the mussels and cook over high heat, shaking the pan, for 5 minutes until opened. Discard any that do not open. Strain the liquid and reserve. Let the mussels cool, then remove from their shells. Preheat the oven to moderately hot 190°C (375°F/Gas 5).

2 **To make Tomato Sauce:** Heat the remaining oil in a pan. Add the garlic and fry until golden. Add the wine and reserved liquid and simmer gently for 5 minutes. Mix the tomato paste (tomato puree) with 3 tablespoons water, then whisk into the simmering liquid. Simmer for a further 10 minutes and season to taste with salt and pepper.

3 **To make White Sauce:** Melt the butter in a pan. Add the flour and cook for 1 minute. Very gradually stir in the milk over low heat until the sauce thickens. Season.

4 Combine the Tomato Sauce and mussels and pour into four 1-cup (250 ml/8½ fl oz) ramekins. Spoon over the White Sauce.

Sprinkle with the combined cheeses and bake for 20 minutes. Serve with crusty bread.

BEEF OLIVES WITH ARTICHOKE STUFFING

Preparation time:
20 minutes

Total cooking time:
50 minutes

Serves 4

INGREDIENTS

- 8 slices beef topside (top round – about 80 g/2¾ oz each slice)
- 100 g (3½ oz) prosciutto, finely chopped
- 50 g (1¾ oz) butter, melted
- 4 artichoke hearts
- 2 tablespoons chopped fresh thyme
- plain (all-purpose) flour, for coating
- ⅓ cup (80 ml/2¾ fl oz) dry white wine
- ½ cup (125 ml/4¼ fl oz) beef stock (broth)

1 Flatten each beef slice with a meat mallet (or rolling pin) until wafer thin. Mix together the prosciutto and 1 tablespoon of the butter and spread over the beef slices. Roughly chop each artichoke into quarters and arrange the pieces evenly over the prosciutto. Sprinkle with thyme and salt and pepper to taste.

2 Roll up the beef slices around the stuffing. Tie each Beef Olive with string to hold it together.

3 Heat the remaining butter in a frying pan. Roll the Beef Olives in a little flour, shake off the excess and fry until browned. Add the wine and the beef stock (broth), then cover and cook for 45 minutes, or until tender. Turn the meat several times during cooking.

4 Remove the Beef Olives with a slotted spoon, cover and keep warm. Return the pan to the heat and reduce the sauce until slightly thickened, if necessary. Season to taste with salt and black pepper. Remove the string from the Beef Olives and pour the sauce over before serving.

NOTE: To make beef stock (broth) at home, bake 2 kg (4 lb 7 oz) beef bones at 210°C (415°F/Gas 6–7) for 30 minutes, then simmer in a large pan with chopped carrots, onions, celery, bouquet garni and 3 litres (3.2 US qt/2.6 UK qt) water for 4 hours. Ready-made stock (broth) is very convenient but can be salty – try using half stock (broth), half water.

BAKED TROUT WITH FENNEL AND WATER CHESTNUTS

Preparation time:
20 minutes

Total cooking time:
20–30 minutes

Serves 4

INGREDIENTS

- 4 whole small trout, cleaned and gutted
- 1 tablespoon sea salt
- 1 teaspoon cracked black pepper
- 2 fennel bulbs, trimmed and thinly sliced
- 230 g (8¼ oz) canned water chestnuts, drained
- ½ cup (125 ml/4¼ fl oz) fresh lemon juice
- ½ cup (125 ml/4¼ fl oz) dry white wine

1 Preheat the oven to moderate 180°C (350°F/Gas 4). Arrange the trout, side by side, in a large baking dish, and sprinkle with sea salt and pepper.

2 Top with the sliced fennel and water chestnuts. Pour over the lemon juice and wine and cover with foil.

3 Bake for 20–30 minutes, or until the fish flakes with a fork and the fennel is tender, then remove the foil and serve immediately.

PORK WITH MUSTARD AND CREAM SAUCE

Preparation time:
10 minutes

Total cooking time:
25 minutes

Serves 4

INGREDIENTS

- 2 tablespoons olive oil
- 4 pork leg steaks
- 1 onion, sliced into rings
- 2 cloves garlic, crushed
- ½ cup (125 ml/4¼ fl oz) white wine
- 1 cup (250 ml/8½ fl oz) cream
- 2 tablespoons wholegrain mustard
- 2 tablespoons chopped parsley

1 Heat the oil in a large frying pan; cook the pork for 3–4 minutes each side. Transfer to a plate and set aside.

2 Reduce the heat and add the onion. Cook until soft, then add the garlic and cook for 1 minute further. Add the wine and simmer until the liquid is reduced by half.

3 Stir in the cream and mustard and simmer gently for 5 minutes. Add the pork and simmer for a further 5 minutes. Stir in the parsley and season to taste. Serve immediately, with the sauce spooned over the pork.

CHICKEN MARSALA

Preparation time:
10 minutes

Total cooking time:
25 minutes

Serves 4

INGREDIENTS

- 4 chicken breast fillets
- 2 tablespoons oil
- 60 g (2 oz) butter
- 1 clove garlic, crushed
- 2 cups (500 ml/17 fl oz) chicken stock (broth)
- ⅓ cup (80 ml/2¾ fl oz) Marsala
- 2 teaspoons plain (all-purpose) flour
- 3 tablespoons cream
- 2 teaspoons Worcestershire sauce

1 Trim the chicken of excess fat and sinew. Heat the oil in a heavy-based frying pan and add the chicken. Cook over medium heat for 4 minutes on each side, or until cooked through and lightly golden. Remove the chicken, cover loosely with foil and keep warm. Drain off any fat from the pan.

2 Add the butter and garlic to the pan and stir over medium heat for 2 minutes. Add the combined stock (broth) and Marsala and bring to the boil. Reduce the heat and simmer for 10 minutes, or until the liquid has reduced by half.

3 Blend together the flour, cream and Worcestershire sauce; add a little of the hot liquid and blend to a paste. Add this to the pan and then stir over medium heat until the sauce boils and thickens. Season to taste with salt and black pepper and then pour over the chicken fillets. Delicious with pasta.

VARIATION: Marsala is a sweet wine and so makes a sweet-tasting sauce. Port or any dry red wine can be used instead. Boiling wine evaporates the alcohol, leaving the flavour but not the intoxicating qualities. Chicken thighs or drumsticks can be used instead of breast fillets.

HINT: Blending the flour to a paste first prevents lumps forming when it is added to the sauce.

LEG OF LAMB WITH PANCETTA STUFFING

Preparation time:
30 minutes

Total cooking time:
1 hour 45 minutes

Serves 6

INGREDIENTS

- 60 g (2 oz) pancetta, chopped
- 60 g (2 oz) mild Provolone cheese, chopped
- 2 tablespoons grated Parmesan
- ⅓ cup (25 g/¾ oz) fresh breadcrumbs
- 3 tablespoons chopped fresh flat-leaf parsley
- 2 teaspoons chopped fresh rosemary
- 2 spring (green) onions, chopped
- 1 egg plus 1 yolk, lightly beaten

- 1.5 kg (3 lb 5 oz) boned leg of lamb (ask your butcher to do this)
- 3 tablespoons olive oil
- 1 onion, chopped
- 1 carrot, chopped
- 1 celery stick (rib), chopped
- 1 cup (250 ml/8½ fl oz) dry white wine
- 1 tablespoon plain (all-purpose) flour

1 Preheat the oven to moderately hot 200°C (400°F/Gas 6). Combine the pancetta, cheeses, breadcrumbs, herbs, spring (green) onions and enough beaten egg to form a stuffing that just comes together. Season with pepper.

2 Fill the lamb leg with stuffing, fold over the ends and secure with wooden skewers or string.

3 Heat the oil in a large deep pan and brown the lamb all over. Transfer to a baking dish and sprinkle with salt and pepper. Reheat the pan and add the onion, carrot and celery; toss over the heat for 2 minutes. Add the wine, let the bubbles subside, then pour over the lamb. Bake for 1½ hours, or until tender, turning once or twice.

4 Remove the meat from the dish
and leave, loosely covered, for
10 minutes before slicing. Strain
the pan juices into a jug and skim
off the fat; add water to make up
1½ cups (375 ml/13 fl oz). Heat
the flour in a small pan until

beginning to brown, remove
from the heat and slowly whisk in
the pan juices until smooth.
Return to the heat and whisk
until the sauce boils and thickens.
Return the vegetables to the
sauce and drizzle over the meat.

LAMB CUTLETS WITH SAGE

Preparation time:
25 minutes

Total cooking time:
1 hour 20 minutes

Serves 4–6

INGREDIENTS

- 8 lamb cutlets
- 2–3 tablespoons plain (all-purpose) flour
- 30 g (1 oz) butter
- 2 tablespoons olive oil
- 75 g (2⅔ oz) sliced ham, cut into strips
- ½ cup (125 ml/4¼ fl oz) dry white wine
- 8 fresh sage leaves, shredded
- 2 teaspoons chopped fresh rosemary
- 1 cup (250 ml/8½ fl oz) beef stock (broth)
- freshly ground black pepper

1 Trim any fat from the lamb cutlets and then toss in flour. Shake off the excess flour.

2 Heat the butter and 1 tablespoon of the oil in a large baking dish. When foaming, add the lamb cutlets in a single layer and cook until browned on both sides. Drain on paper towels. Wipe the pan clean, then add the remaining oil and the ham; toss over the heat for a few minutes.

3 Return the cutlets to the pan, then pour in the wine with the herbs. Simmer, uncovered, until most of the liquid has evaporated. Add the stock (broth) and black pepper. Bring back to the boil, reduce the heat and simmer, covered (with foil if necessary), for about 1 hour, or until the cutlets are tender, turning once during cooking.

4 Transfer the cutlets to a serving dish and keep warm. If the pan juices are very thin, simmer uncovered until thickened. Season with salt to taste, if necessary, then pour over the cutlets. Garnish with fresh sage.

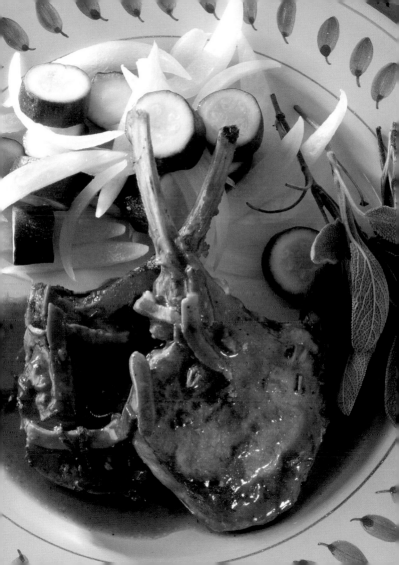

PESTO LAMB CUTLETS

Preparation time:
40 minutes + chilling

Total cooking time:
20 minutes

Serves 4

INGREDIENTS

- 12 lamb cutlets
- 1 egg
- 3 tablespoons pesto
- 1 teaspoon wholegrain mustard
- 2 tablespoons cornflour (cornstarch)
- 1 cup (80 g/2¾ oz) fresh breadcrumbs
- ⅓ cup (35 g/1¼ oz) grated Parmesan
- ⅓ cup (50 g/1¾ oz) pine nuts, finely chopped

1 Trim any fat from the cutlets and scrape the flesh from the bone to give them a nice shape. Whisk together the egg, pesto, mustard and cornflour (cornstarch).

2 Mix the breadcrumbs, Parmesan and pine nuts in a bowl. Dip each cutlet into the pesto then breadcrumb mixtures. Chill for 30 minutes.

3 Shallow-fry the cutlets in oil, in batches, for 5 minutes each side.

NOTE: To make pesto, process 2 bunches basil leaves, 4 tablespoons toasted pine nuts, 2 crushed garlic cloves and 4 tablespoons grated Parmesan until finely chopped. Still processing, slowly add 4 tablespoons olive oil in a stream, until well mixed.

PAN-FRIED FISH

Preparation time:
Nil

Total cooking time:
8 minutes

Serves 4

INGREDIENTS

- plain (all-purpose) flour, for dusting
- olive oil
- 4 white fish steaks, such as swordfish or blue-eyed cod

1 Sift the flour together with a little salt and pepper onto a dinner plate. Coat both sides of the fish steaks with seasoned flour, shaking off the excess.

2 Heat about 3 mm (⅛ inch) oil in a frying pan until very hot. Put the fish into the hot oil immediately and cook for 3 minutes on one side, then turn and cook the other side for 2 minutes, or until the coating is crisp and well browned. Reduce the heat to low and cook for a further 2–3 minutes, until the flesh flakes easily with a fork.

3 Remove from the pan and drain briefly on paper towels, then serve straight away, perhaps with lemon wedges, sautéed potatoes and a salad.

NOTE: Cook the fish in batches, if necessary. Don't overcrowd the pan or the temperature will be reduced.

BRAISED LAMB SHANKS

Preparation time:
30 minutes

Total cooking time:
2 hours 50 minutes

Serves 4–6

INGREDIENTS

- 2 tablespoons plain (all-purpose) flour
- freshly ground black pepper
- 4 lamb shanks, cut into short lengths
- 2 tablespoons oil
- 2 cloves garlic, crushed
- 1 large onion, chopped
- 1 large carrot, chopped
- ⅔ cup (170 ml/5¾ fl oz) dry white wine
- ⅔ cup (170 ml/5¾ fl oz) beef stock (broth)

- 425 g (15 oz) can tomatoes
- 3 tablespoons tomato paste (tomato puree)
- ½ teaspoon caster (berry) sugar

GREMOLATA
- ⅓ cup (7 g/¼ oz) fresh parsley
- 1 clove garlic, crushed
- 2 teaspoons grated lemon rind

1 Preheat the oven to moderate 180°C (350°F/Gas 4). Lightly grease a 12-cup (3-litre/ 3.2 US qt/2.6 UK qt) baking dish. Combine the flour and pepper on a sheet of greaseproof paper and lightly coat the meat. Shake off the excess.

2 Heat the oil in a heavy-based pan. Brown the meat on both sides over medium-high heat; drain on paper towels. Transfer to the baking dish.

3 Add the garlic and onion to the pan and cook, stirring, until just soft. Add the carrot, wine, stock (broth), crushed tomatoes, tomato paste (tomato puree) and sugar. Bring to the boil, reduce the heat and simmer for 5 minutes. Spoon over the meat, cover with foil and bake for 2 hours. Uncover and bake for a further 30 minutes, or until tender.

4 To make Gremolata: Finely chop the parsley, then mix with the garlic and rind. Just before serving, sprinkle Gremolata over the meat.

STORAGE TIME: Cook up to 1 day ahead and keep, covered, in the refrigerator, or freeze for 1 month. Make Gremolata just before serving.

BEEF WITH PROSCIUTTO AND MUSHROOMS

Preparation time:
15 minutes

Total cooking time:
25 minutes

Serves 4

INGREDIENTS

- 2 tablespoons olive oil
- 200 g (7 oz) button mushrooms, stalks trimmed
- 60 g (2 oz) sliced prosciutto, cut into wide strips
- 4 thick slices beef scotch fillet or rib-eye fillet steaks
- 2 cloves garlic, crushed
- 2 tablespoons chopped fresh flat-leaf parsley
- ¼ cup (60 ml/2 fl oz) dry white wine
- ½ cup (125 ml/4¼ fl oz) cream

1 Preheat the oven to moderately hot 200°C (400°F/Gas 6). Heat the oil in a deep ovenproof frying pan (large enough to hold the beef steaks in one layer, without overlapping). Add the mushrooms and prosciutto and toss until the mushrooms start to brown.

2 Layer the steaks over the mushrooms, sprinkle with garlic and parsley, then pour over the wine. Bring to the boil, reduce the heat, then cover the pan (with a lid or tightly with foil) and bake for 10–15 minutes, or until the steaks are cooked to taste.

3 Set the steaks aside to keep warm. Heat the pan on the hotplate, add the cream and boil for 3–5 minutes, or until thickened slightly; pour over the steaks and serve immediately.

NOTE: Flat-leaf parsley is also known as Italian or continental parsley.

OCTOPUS IN FRESH TOMATO SAUCE

Preparation time:
20 minutes

Total cooking time:
1 hour 10 minutes

Serves 4–6

INGREDIENTS

- 1 kg (2 lb 3 oz) baby octopus
- 2 tablespoons olive oil
- ⅓ cup (80 ml/2¾ fl oz) dry white wine
- 500 g (1 lb 2 oz) ripe tomatoes, peeled and chopped
- 4 pickling onions, peeled and quartered
- 1 clove garlic, chopped
- 2 tablespoons chopped fresh flat-leaf parsley

1 Wash the octopus and cut the heads off. Cut open the heads and remove the guts. Wash the heads and drain. Remove the beaks and cut the tentacles into sets of four.

2 Heat the oil in a large pan until very hot, add the octopus and toss over high heat for about 10 minutes, or until the octopus is opaque and the pan almost dry. Add the wine and simmer, uncovered, until most of the liquid has evaporated, then add the tomato and onions. Bring to the boil, then reduce the heat and simmer over low heat for 45 minutes to 1 hour, or until tender.

3 Serve hot or warm, sprinkled with the combined chopped garlic and parsley and lots of black pepper.

NOTE: To peel tomatoes, cut a cross in the base, plunge in boiling water then into cold. Peel the skin from the cross.

TROUT WITH LEEK AND CAPER SAUCE

Preparation time:
10 minutes

Total cooking time:
10 minutes

Serves 4

INGREDIENTS

- 45 g (1⅔ oz) melted butter
- 4 thick ocean trout fillets
  (about 155 g/5½ oz each)

LEEK AND CAPER SAUCE
- 50 g (1¾ oz) butter
- 1 leek, chopped
- 1 cup (250 ml/8½ fl oz) white
  wine (riesling or chardonnay)
- 2 tablespoons capers, drained
- 1 tablespoon chopped
  flat-leaf parsley

1 Brush a shallow oven tray (sheet) with melted butter and put the fish on the tray. Brush with melted butter and grill (broil) under moderate heat, without turning, until the fish is just cooked. Remove and cover loosely with foil to keep warm while making the sauce.

2 **To make Leek and Caper Sauce:** Melt the butter in a pan and cook the leek gently until soft, but not brown. Add the wine and simmer for 3–4 minutes. Add the capers and parsley and salt and pepper to taste, then remove from the heat.

3 Spoon the hot sauce over the fish and serve immediately.

VARIATION: Use salmon fillets or cutlets or any thick white fish instead of trout.

CHICKEN PARMIGIANA

Preparation time:
30 minutes + chilling

Total cooking time:
30 minutes

Serves 4

INGREDIENTS

- 4 chicken breast fillets
- 1 cup (100 g/3½ oz) dry breadcrumbs
- ½ teaspoon dried basil
- ¼ cup (25 g/¾ oz) finely grated fresh Parmesan
- plain (all-purpose) flour, for coating
- 1 egg, lightly beaten
- 1 tablespoon milk
- olive oil, for frying
- 1 cup (250 g/8¾ oz) good-quality ready-made tomato pasta (marinara) sauce
- ½ cup (50 g/1¼ oz) finely grated fresh Parmesan, extra
- 100 g (3½ oz) mozzarella, thinly sliced

1 Trim the meat of any excess fat and sinew. Place between sheets of plastic wrap and flatten with a meat mallet to 5 mm (¼ inch) thick. Nick the edges to prevent curling. Combine the breadcrumbs, basil and Parmesan on a sheet of greaseproof paper.

2 Coat the chicken breast fillets in flour, shaking off the excess. Working with one at a time, dip the fillets into the combined egg and milk, then coat with the breadcrumb mixture. Lightly shake off the excess. Refrigerate for 30 minutes to firm the coating.

3 Preheat the oven to moderate 180°C (350°F/Gas 4). Heat the oil in a frying pan and brown the chicken breast fillets over medium heat for 2 minutes each side, in batches if necessary. Drain on paper towels.

4 Spread half the pasta (marinara) sauce into a shallow ovenproof dish. Arrange the chicken breast fillets on top in a single layer and spoon over the remaining sauce.

Top with the Parmesan cheese and mozzarella and bake for 20 minutes, or until the cheeses are melted and golden brown. Serve immediately.

PANNA COTTA WITH RUBY SAUCE

Preparation time:
20 minutes + chilling

Total cooking time:
20 minutes

Serves 6

INGREDIENTS

- 1½ cups (375 ml/13 fl oz) milk
- 3 teaspoons gelatine
- 1½ cups (375 ml/13 fl oz) cream
- ⅓ cup (90 g/3¼ oz) caster (berry) sugar
- 2 tablespoons amaretto (almond-flavoured) liqueur

RUBY SAUCE
- 1 cup (250 g/8¾ oz) caster (berry) sugar
- 1 cinnamon stick
- 1 cup fresh or frozen raspberries
- ½ cup (125 ml/4¼ fl oz) good-quality red wine

1 Use your fingertips to lightly smear the inside of 6 individual 150 ml (5 fl oz) moulds with almond or light olive oil. Place 3 tablespoons of the milk in a small bowl and sprinkle with gelatine; leave to dissolve for a few minutes.

2 Put the remaining milk in a pan with the cream and sugar and heat gently while stirring, until almost boiling. Remove the pan from the heat; whisk the gelatine into the cream mixture and whisk until dissolved. Leave to cool for 5 minutes and then stir in the amaretto.

3 Pour the mixture into the moulds and chill until set (about 4 hours). Unmould and serve with Ruby Sauce.

4 **To make Ruby Sauce:** Place the sugar and 1 cup (250 ml/ 8½ fl oz) water in a pan and stir over medium heat until the sugar has completely dissolved (do not allow to boil). Add the cinnamon stick and simmer for 5 minutes. Add the raspberries and wine and boil rapidly for 5 minutes. Remove the cinnamon stick and push the sauce through a sieve; discard the seeds. Cool and then chill the sauce in the refrigerator before serving.

NOTE: If you prefer, replace the amaretto with ½ teaspoon almond extract. The Panna Cotta will be a little firmer. This is delicious, and traditionally Italian, with fresh figs.

TIRAMISU

Preparation time:
30 minutes + chilling

Total cooking time:
Nil

Serves 6–8

INGREDIENTS

- 3 cups (750 ml/26 fl oz) strong black coffee, cooled
- 3 tablespoons dark rum
- 2 eggs, separated
- 3 tablespoons caster (berry) sugar
- 250 g (8¼ oz) mascarpone
- 1 cup cream (250 ml/8½ fl oz), whipped
- 16 large savoiardi biscuits (cookies)
- 2 teaspoons dark cocoa powder

1 Put the coffee and rum in a bowl. Using electric beaters, beat the egg yolks and sugar in a small bowl for 3 minutes, or until thick and pale. Add the mascarpone and beat until just combined. Fold in the whipped cream with a metal spoon.

2 Beat the egg whites until soft peaks form. Fold quickly and lightly into the cream mixture with a metal spoon, trying not to lose the volume.

3 Dip half the biscuits (cookies), one at a time, into the coffee mixture; drain off any excess and arrange in the base of a deep serving dish. Spread half the cream mixture over the biscuits (cookies).

4 Dip the remaining biscuits (cookies) and repeat the layers. Smooth the surface and dust liberally with cocoa powder. Refrigerate for 2 hours, or until firm, to allow the flavours to develop. Delicious served with fresh fruit.

STORAGE TIME: Tiramisu may be made up to 8 hours in advance. Refrigerate until required.

CHOCOLATE RICOTTA TART

Preparation time:
20 minutes + chilling

Total cooking time:
1 hour

Serves 8–10

INGREDIENTS

- 1½ cups (185 g/6½ oz) plain (all-purpose) flour
- 100 g (3½ oz) cold butter, chopped
- 2 tablespoons caster (berry) sugar
- 1 tablespoon butter, melted

FILLING

- 1.25 kg (2 lb 12 oz) ricotta cheese
- ½ cup (125 g/4⅓ oz) caster (berry) sugar
- 2 tablespoons plain (all-purpose) flour
- 125 g (4⅓ oz) chocolate, finely chopped
- 2 teaspoons coffee essence
- 4 egg yolks
- 40 g (1½ oz) chocolate, extra
- ½ teaspoon vegetable oil

1 Make sweet shortcrust (pie) pastry by sifting the flour into a large bowl and adding the butter. Rub the butter into the flour with your fingertips, until fine and crumbly. Stir in the sugar. Add 3 tablespoons cold water and cut with a knife to form a dough, adding a little more water if necessary. Turn out onto a lightly floured surface and gather together into a ball. Brush a 25 cm (10 inch) springform tin with melted butter. Roll out the dough to line the tin, coming about two-thirds of the way up the side. Cover and refrigerate while making the filling.

2 **To make Filling:** Mix together the ricotta, sugar, flour and a pinch of salt until smooth. Stir in the chocolate, coffee essence and yolks until well mixed. Spoon into the chilled pastry shell and smooth. Chill for 30 minutes, or until firm. Preheat the oven to moderate 180°C (350°F/Gas 4).

3 Put the tin on a baking tray (sheet). Bake for 1 hour, or until firm. Leave to cool before removing the sides from the tin. Melt the extra chocolate and stir in the oil. With a fork, flick thin drizzles of melted chocolate over the tart. Cool completely before cutting.

NOTE: The tart may crack during baking but this will not be noticeable when it cools and is decorated.

HAZELNUT PUDDINGS WITH CHOCOLATE CREAM SAUCE AND HONEY ZABAGLIONE

Preparation time:
40 minutes

Total cooking time:
40 minutes

Serves 8

INGREDIENTS

- 30 g (1 oz) butter, melted
- ½ cup (55 g/2 oz) ground hazelnuts
- 125 g (4⅓ oz) butter
- ½ cup (125 g/4⅓ oz) caster (berry) sugar
- 3 eggs, lightly beaten
- 2 cups (250 g/8¾ oz) self-raising flour, sifted
- ½ cup (60 g/2 oz) sultanas (golden raisins)
- ⅓ cup (80 ml/2¾ fl oz) brandy
- ⅓ cup (80 ml/2¾ fl oz) buttermilk
- white chocolate shavings, to decorate

CHOCOLATE CREAM SAUCE
- 1 cup (250 ml/8½ fl oz) cream
- 30 g (1 oz) butter
- 200 g (oz) dark (semi-sweet) chocolate, chopped

HONEY ZABAGLIONE
- 3 large egg yolks
- 3 tablespoons honey
- 2 tablespoons brandy
- ½ cup (125 ml/4¼ fl oz) cream

1 Preheat the oven to moderate 180°C (350°F/Gas 4). Brush eight, ½-cup (125 ml/4¼ fl oz) ovenproof ramekins with melted butter and coat with the ground hazelnuts, shaking off the excess. Beat together the butter and sugar with electric beaters until

light and creamy. Add the eggs gradually, beating well after each addition. Fold in the flour, sultanas (golden raisins), brandy and buttermilk. Spoon into the ramekins, cover with greased foil and secure with string.

2 Place the puddings in a large baking dish and pour in enough water to come three-quarters of the way up the sides of the ramekins. Bake for 25 minutes, topping up with more water if necessary. Test with a skewer before removing the ramekins from the pan – the skewer should come out clean when inserted into the centre of the pudding.

3 **To make Chocolate Cream Sauce:** Put the cream, butter and chocolate in a small pan and stir over low heat until melted and smooth. Remove from the heat and set aside.

4 **To make Honey Zabaglione:** Beat the egg yolks until thick and pale. Place the bowl over a pan of barely simmering water and beat in the honey. Beat for about 5 minutes, until thickened. Remove from the heat, cool to room temperature and stir in the brandy. Beat the cream in a small bowl until firm peaks form, then fold into the egg mixture.

5 Spread Chocolate Cream Sauce over half of each serving plate. Pour Zabaglione onto the other half. Unmould the warm pudding onto the centre of the plate and decorate with curls of white chocolate.

HINT: Make chocolate shavings by simply running over the top of the chocolate block with a vegetable peeler. Or make chocolate curls by melting the chocolate and spreading in a thin layer over a cool smooth surface (such as a marble board). When the chocolate has set, scrape off curls with the edge of a sharp knife.

CHILLED ORANGE CREAMS

Preparation time:
30 minutes + chilling

Total cooking time:
5 minutes

Serves 6

INGREDIENTS

- ½ cup (125 ml/4¼ fl oz) juice of blood oranges
- 3 teaspoons gelatine
- 4 egg yolks
- ½ cup (125 g/4⅓ oz) caster (berry) sugar
- 1¼ cups (315 ml/11¼ fl oz) milk
- 1 teaspoon finely grated blood orange rind
- 1 cup (250 ml/8½ fl oz) cream

1 Put a large bowl in the freezer and chill. Put a few drops of almond or light olive oil on your fingertips and lightly grease the insides of six ½-cup (125 ml/ 4¼ fl oz) moulds. Put the orange juice in a small bowl and sprinkle with gelatine; set aside.

2 Whisk the yolks and sugar in a small bowl until thick. Heat the milk and rind in a pan and gradually pour onto the egg mixture while whisking. Return to the pan and stir until the custard coats the back of the spoon – do not allow it to boil. Add the gelatine mixture and stir to dissolve.

3 Pour the mixture immediately through a strainer into the chilled bowl. Cool, stirring occasionally, until beginning to thicken. Whip the cream into soft peaks and fold into the custard. Spoon into the moulds and chill to set. Serve with cream, if liked.

VARIATION: Blood oranges have a short season but they give the best colour. You could use navel or Valencia oranges, or mandarins.

SICILIAN CHEESECAKE

Preparation time:
45 minutes + chilling

Total cooking time:
1 hour 25 minutes

Serves 8

INGREDIENTS

- 2 cups (250 g/8¾ oz) plain (all-purpose) flour
- 160 g (5⅔ oz) butter, chopped
- ¼ cup (60 g/2 oz) caster (berry) sugar
- 1 teaspoon grated lemon rind
- 1 egg, lightly beaten

RICOTTA FILLING
- ½ cup (60 g/2 oz) raisins (dark raisins), chopped
- ⅓ cup (80 ml/2¾ fl oz) Marsala
- 500 g (1 lb 2 oz) fresh ricotta
- ½ cup (125 g/4⅓ oz) caster (berry) sugar
- 1 tablespoon plain (all-purpose) flour
- 4 eggs, separated
- ½ cup (125 ml/4¼ fl oz) cream

1 Lightly grease a 26 cm (10½ inch) round springform tin. Sift the flour and a pinch of salt into a large bowl and rub in the butter. Add the sugar, rind, egg and a little water if necessary and, using a knife, cut through until a rough dough forms. Press together into a ball.

2 Roll out the dough on a lightly floured surface to line the base and side of the tin; chill for 30 minutes. Preheat the oven to moderately hot 190°C (375°F/ Gas 5). Prick the pastry base, line with baking paper and fill with dried beans or rice. Bake for 15 minutes, then remove the beans and paper and bake for 8 minutes, or until pastry is dry. If the base puffs up, gently press down with the beans in the paper. Allow to cool. Reduce the oven to warm 160°C (315°F/Gas 2–3).

3 **To make Filling:** Put the raisins (dark raisins) and Marsala in a small bowl, cover and leave to soak. Push the ricotta through a sieve. Beat the ricotta and caster (berry) sugar with a wooden spoon until combined. Add the flour and egg yolks, then the cream and undrained raisins (dark raisins) and mix well. In a small bowl, beat the egg whites until soft peaks form and gently fold into the ricotta mixture in two batches.

4 Pour the filling into the pastry case and bake for 1 hour, or until just set. Check during cooking and cover with foil if the pastry is overbrowning. Cool a little in the oven with the door ajar to prevent sinking. Serve warm with whipped cream.

ALMOND CITRUS TART

Preparation time:
40 minutes + chilling

Total cooking time:
1 hour

Serves 6–8

INGREDIENTS

- 2 cups (250 g/8¾ oz) plain (all-purpose) flour, sifted
- ¼ cup (60 g/2 oz) caster (berry) sugar
- 125 g (4⅓ oz) butter, softened
- 1 teaspoon finely grated lemon rind
- 2 egg yolks

FILLING
- 350 g (12¼ oz) fresh ricotta, sieved
- ⅓ cup (90 g/3¼ oz) caster (berry) sugar
- 3 eggs, well beaten
- 1 tablespoon grated lemon rind
- ½ cup (80 g/2¾ oz) blanched almonds, finely chopped
- 3 tablespoons flaked almonds
- icing (powdered) sugar, to dust

1 Combine the flour, sugar and a pinch of salt in a large bowl. Make a well in the centre and add the butter, rind and yolks. Work the flour into the centre with the fingertips of one hand until a smooth dough forms (add a little more flour if necessary). Wrap in plastic wrap and chill for 1 hour.

2 **To make Filling:** Using electric beaters, beat the ricotta and sugar together. Add the eggs gradually, beating well after each addition. Add the rind, beating briefly to combine, and then stir in the chopped almonds.

3 Preheat the oven to moderate 180°C (350°F/Gas 4). Brush a 20 cm (8 inch) deep fluted flan tin with melted butter. Roll out the pastry on a lightly floured surface and line the prepared tin, removing the excess pastry. Pour in the filling and smooth the top. Sprinkle with the flaked almonds and bake for 55 minutes to 1 hour, or until lightly golden and set.

4 Cool to room temperature and carefully remove the sides from the tin. Dust with icing (powdered) sugar to serve at room temperature or chilled.

LEMON SYRUP CAKE

Preparation time:
20 minutes

Total cooking time:
45 minutes

Serves 8

INGREDIENTS

- 1 cup (125 g/4⅓ oz) plain
  (all-purpose) flour
- ¾ teaspoon baking powder
- ¼ teaspoon bicarbonate of soda
  (baking soda)
- 50 g (1¾ oz) unsalted butter
- ½ cup (125 g/4⅓ oz) caster
  (berry) sugar
- 2 eggs
- ⅓ cup (80 ml/2¾ fl oz) milk
- 3 tablespoons ground almonds
- 2 tablespoons grated lemon rind

SYRUP
- 100 g (3½ oz) caster (berry) sugar
- ⅓ cup (80 ml/2¾ fl oz) fresh
  lemon juice

1 Preheat the oven to moderate
   180°C (350°F/Gas 4). Grease
   and line a 20 cm (8 inch)
   springform tin. Sift the flour,
   baking powder, bicarbonate of
   soda (baking soda) and a pinch
   of salt into a bowl.

2 In a separate bowl, beat the
   butter, sugar and eggs until light
   and creamy (the mixture may
   appear curdled). Fold in the
   flour mixture, then gently stir
   in the milk, almonds and lemon
   rind. Spoon into the tin and bake
   for 30–35 minutes, or until a
   skewer comes out clean. Make
   holes in the top of the cake with
   the skewer.

3 **To make Syrup:** Put the sugar
   and lemon juice in a small pan
   and stir over a low heat until
   syrupy; keep warm. Pour the
   syrup over the hot cake. Cool on
   a wire rack, then turn out of the
   tin to serve.

RICOTTA POTS
WITH RASPBERRIES

Preparation time:
20 minutes

Total cooking time:
25 minutes

Serves 4

INGREDIENTS

- 4 eggs, separated
- ½ cup (125 g/4⅓ oz) caster (berry) sugar
- 350 g (12¼ oz) fresh ricotta
- ¼ cup (35 g/1¼ oz) finely chopped pistachio nuts
- 1 teaspoon grated lemon rind
- 2 tablespoons lemon juice
- 1 tablespoon vanilla sugar (see NOTE)
- 200 g (7 oz) fresh raspberries

1 Preheat the oven to moderate 180°C (350°F/Gas 4). Beat the egg yolks and sugar in a small bowl until pale and creamy. Transfer to a large bowl and add the ricotta, pistachio nuts, lemon rind and juice and mix well.

2 In a separate bowl, whisk the egg whites into stiff peaks. Beat in the vanilla sugar, then fold into the ricotta mixture, stirring until just combined.

3 Lightly grease 4 individual, 1-cup (250 ml/8½ fl oz) ramekins. Divide the raspberries among the dishes and spoon the ricotta filling over the top. Place on an oven tray (sheet) and bake for 20–25 minutes, or until puffed and lightly browned. Serve immediately, dusted with a little icing (powdered) sugar.

NOTE: You can buy vanilla sugar at the supermarket or make your own. Split a whole vanilla bean in half lengthways and place in a jar of caster (berry) sugar (about 1 kg/ 2 lb 3 oz). Leave for at least 4 days before using.

ICE-CREAM CASSATA

Preparation time:
30 minutes + chilling
and overnight freezing

Total cooking time:
Nil

Serves 8–10

INGREDIENTS

- 250 g (8¾ oz) glacé (glazed) fruit (such as cherries, apricots or pineapple), finely chopped
- ⅓ cup (40 g/1½ oz) slivered almonds, finely chopped
- ⅓ cup (80 ml/2¾ fl oz) triple sec or other orange-flavoured liqueur

- 2 litres (2.1 US qt/1.75 UK qt) good-quality vanilla ice-cream, softened slightly
- 1¼ cups (185 g/6½ oz) unsalted pistachio nuts, shelled and finely chopped

1 Cover the chopped glacé (glazed) fruit and almonds with the liqueur and soak for 10 minutes. Put a 9-cup (2.25 litre/2.4 US qt/ 2 UK qt) pudding basin in the refrigerator. While the pudding basin is chilling, divide the softened ice-cream in half and fold the pistachio nuts through one half. If it begins to melt, return the ice-cream to the freezer until it is firm enough to spread.

2 When the basin is very cold, line it with a layer of the pistachio ice-cream to three-quarters of the way up the side (use a spoon, dipped in warm water occasionally, to help spread it evenly). Place in the freezer to re-set.

3 Combine the remaining ice-cream with the soaked glacé (glazed) fruit and almonds. Mix until well combined. (Return to the freezer if the ice-cream has softened too much to spread.) Remove the basin from the freezer and spoon in the ice-cream and fruit mixture. Smooth the surface and return to the freezer overnight, or until completely set.

4 Turn out onto a chilled platter and cut into wedges to serve.

STORAGE TIME: Will keep frozen for up to one month.

HINT: An easy way to turn out the Cassata is to lay a hot damp cloth over the basin and keep reheating the cloth until the basin lifts away. Try not to melt the outside of the Cassata too much.

INDEX

A

Agnolotti with
Alfredo Sauce 90
Almond Citrus Tart 166–167
Angel Hair Pasta
with Scallops 78
Asparagus with Parmesan 22

B

Baked Mushrooms 24
Baked Polenta with
Three Cheeses 108–109
Baked Ricotta 6–7
Baked Trout with Fennel
and Water Chestnuts 130
Beef Olives with
Artichoke Stuffing 128–129
Beef with Prosciutto
and Mushrooms 146
Braised Lamb Shanks 144–145
Broccoli and Pine
Nut Soup 40
Bruschetta with
Mediterranean Toppings 8–9

C

Caponata 20
Caraway Polenta
with Leeks 112
Carrot and Pumpkin
Risotto 106
Cheese and Spinach
Pancakes 26–27
Chicken Marsala 134
Chicken Parmigiana 152–153
Chilled Orange Creams 162
Chocolate Ricotta Tart 158–159
Creamy Pasta Bake 66
Creamy Tomato and
Bacon Pasta 70

F

Fennel with Pecorino
Cheese 28
Fettucine with Spinach
and Roast Tomato 86–87
Fish and Vegetable Rolls 18
Fresh Fettucine with
Seared Tuna 74

G

Garlic and Chilli
  Oil Spaghetti 76
Grape and Walnut Salad 12

H

Ham and Cheese Calzone 52
Hazelnut Puddings with
  Chocolate Cream
  Sauce and Honey
  Zabaglione 160–161

I

Ice-Cream Cassata 172–173

L

Lamb Cutlets with Sage 138
Leg of Lamb with
  Pancetta Stuffing 136–137
Lemon Syrup Cake 168
Linguine with Ham, Artichoke
  and Lemon Sauce 72

M

Minestrone 38
Mushroom and
  Pancetta Risotto 102
Mushroom and
  Ricotta Cannelloni 98

Mushrooms in
  Tomato Sauce 30
Mussels in Two Sauces 126–127

O

Octopus in Fresh
  Tomato Sauce 148
Olive and Lemon
  Lamb Cutlets 116
Olive and Onion Tart 50
Oven-Baked Potato,
  Leek and Olives 114

P

Pan-Fried Fish 142
Panna Cotta with
  Ruby Sauce 154–155
Parmesan Pears 10
Pasta Gnocchi
  with Sausage 58
Pea and Pancetta
  Risotto 104–105
Pesto Lamb Cutlets 140
Polenta with Wild
  Mushrooms 110–111
Pork Scaloppini
  with Lemon Sauce 118
Pork with Mustard
  and Cream Sauce 132

Potato Onion Pizza 46–47
Prawn Saffron
   Risotto 100–101
Prosciutto and
   Spinach Lasagne 96
Pumpkin and Bean Soup 42

R

Ravioli in Roasted
   Vegetable Sauce 88
Rich Cheese Macaroni 68
Ricotta and
   Pasta Timbales 64–65
Ricotta Pots with
   Raspberries 170
Roasted Butternut Sauce
   on Pappardelle 60
Roasted Tomato and
   Oregano Pizza 54–55

S

Seafood Soup 36–37
Sicilian Cheesecake 164–165
Smoked Chicken Linguine 84
Spaghetti Bolognese 56
Spaghetti Marinara 80
Spaghetti Nicoise 92

Spaghetti Primavera 82
Spinach and Pancetta Pie 16–17
Spinach Ravioli with
   Pine Nut Salsa 62
Spring Chicken with
   Honey Glaze 122
Stuffed Calamari 124
Stuffed Sardines 34
Sun-Dried Tomato and
   Salami Pizza 48–49

T

Tiramisu 156
Tomato Ditalini Soup 44
Tortellini with
   Mushroom Sauce 94
Trout with Leek and
   Caper Sauce 150
Tuna Steaks with Warm
   Bean Salad 120

V

Vegetable Boats 14

W

Whitebait Fritters 32